글로벌 기업을 만드는

조직문화와 리더십

김종남(John Kim) 지음

숲

CONTENTS

I

조직문화와
리더십을
이해해야 하는 이유

1. 이 책을 쓴 이유

나의 직업은 조직 개발이며, 조직을 변화시키는 것이 주요 미션이다. 자연스럽게 우리나라의 유수 기업과 중소기업, 그리고 외국계 기업들을 매일 접하게 된다. 그러다 보니 고객사로부터 어떻게 하면 조직을 변화시킬 수 있는지에 대해 문의를 많이 받는다. 기업들의 변화를 위해 고객사의 본사뿐만 아니라 지사와 연구소, 미국, 독일, 태국, 중국, 말레이시아, 인도네시아, 네덜란드, 핀란드, 프랑스, 인도, 베트남 등을 방문하고 세계 50여 개국 이상 출신의 사람들을 워크숍과 코칭을 통해 만나고 이야기를 들어왔다. 그들은 주로 한국의 문화와 한국 기업들의 조직문화, 리더십을 이야기한다. 그 속에서 나는 항상 스스로에게 질문해 왔다. "우리 기업들의 현 주소는 어디쯤일까?"

몇 년 전부터 한국 사회에 '수평적 조직문화'와 '수평적 리더십'이라는 말이 유행하기 시작하여 이제는 진부한 용어가 된 것처럼 느껴진다. 물론 조직의 내면으로 들어가보면 아직 수평적 문화와 리더십을 제대로 실현하는 기업들은 그다지 많지 않을 것이다. 다양한 국가와 기업 경험을 가진 사람들과 이야기를 하다 보면 우리가 추구해야 하는 미래상이 어떠해야 하는지에 대해 나름 생각을 정리할 수 있게 된다. 좀 더 쉽게 말해서 우리 기업들이 추구해야 할 조직문화의 바람직한 수준, 리더십의 바람직한 수준은 어떠해야 할까? 아니 보편타당하게 이 지구상에서 통할 수 있는 수준은 무엇을 말할까? 이에 대한 이야기가 이 책을 쓰게 만들었다.

조직 개발을 전공으로 일하고 있지만, 조직의 바람직한 변화에 있어 특정 기업에 딱 들어 맞는 해답이 존재한다고는 생각하지 않는다. 하지만 우리 기업들이 추구해야 할 이상향이 존재한다는 것은 틀림없다고 생각한다. 세계 유수 기업들과 어깨를 나란히 할 수 있고, 지구촌의 다양한 사람들의 가치를 수용할 수 있고, 이들과 함께 일하고 이들의 도움으로 보다 성장할 수 있는 조직문화와 리더십은 반드시 존재한다고 생각한다. 이를 일러 나는 '글로벌 조직문화와 리더십'이라고 부르며, 이를 어떻게 만들 것인가에 대해 탐구해볼 가치는 충분히 존재한다고 생각한다.

다시 말해, 우리 기업들이 고(高)성과 조직으로 성장하고 세계 시장을 리드하며, 한국 시장이라는 울타리를 넘어서 지속가능한 성장을 하려면 장기적 전략의 또 다른 이름인 글로벌 조직문화를 만들 수 있어야 하고, 이를 낳을 수 있는 리더십을 출현시킬 수 있어야 한다. 전략이 자라는 환경이 조직문화라면, 리더십은 전략도 낳고 문화도 낳기 때문에 그 중요성을 간과할 수 없다. 그런 면에서 글로벌 조직문화를 갖는다는 것은 무엇을 의미하는지, 어떤 환경에서 그런 것들이 탄생할 수 있는지, 그리고 어떤 장애들이 그런 문화와 리더십의 형성을 저해하는지 등을 살펴보고 싶었다. 예를 들어 우리는 우리의 현재 실력만으로도 글로벌 시장에서 상위 경쟁자로 우뚝 설 수 있다고 착각할 수 있지만, 기술과 상품, 서비스는 문화와 리더십의 영역 내에서만 성장할 수 있다는 점을 잊어서는 안된다.

다른 나라 기업의 출신들과 이야기를 하다 보면 우리의 회의 문화와 보고 문화, 끼리끼리 문화, 상급자 우선 문화, 소통 방식, 리더들의 보수 성향 때문에 글로벌 기업으로 성장하는 데 한계가 있다고 한다. 글로벌 시장이 이미 열려 있는데, 우리가 기존에 해왔던 방식들이 우리의 발목을 잡고 있다는 말이다. 우리에게 부족한 오픈 마인드가 글로벌 시장을 놓치게 만드는 장애물이 되고 있다는 것이다. 그런 면에서 글로벌 조직문화와 리더십을 한 번 더 생각해 볼 필요는 글로벌 기업을 꿈꾸는 대한민국의 모든 기업들에 충분하다고 생각한다.

문제는 조직문화와 리더십은 하루 아침에 변하지 않는다는 것이다. 오랜 시간과 고민이 필요하고, 미래를 내다보는 통찰과 거시적인 안목이 필요하다. 그런 측면에서 우리 기업들이 앞으로 글로벌 조직문화와 리더십에 초점을 두고 개선 노력을 해나간다면 바람직한 성장에 한 걸음 더 다가가는 것이라고 생각한다. 글로벌 인재들과 글로벌 기업들을 경험하면서 느끼는 것은 시스템을 구축하는 것은 정말 오랜 시간이 필요하다는 점이다. 차근차근 시간을 갖고 기업의 리더십을 준비하고자 한다면, 그리고 조직의 문화를 변화해 나가고자 한다면 이 책은 작지만 충분히 의미가 있을 것이라고 생각한다.

2. 왜 영어를 사용했는가?

나는 『The Korea Times』에 3년간 60여 편의 칼럼을 기고해 왔다. 우리 기업들의 현장을 방문하여 느낀 점들을 정리하며 어떤 방향으로의 성장이 필요한가에 대해서 기록한 조직 진단 일기와 같은 성격으로 써 왔다. 그 과정에서 많은 분들의 의견을 들을 수 있었다. 특히 영어 공부에 좋다는 말을 많이 들었다. 그런데 다양한 기업들을 방문하여 변화 활동을 하다 보면 영어가 단순히 영어 공부 차원에서가 아니라 글로벌 조직문화와 리더십을 완성하는 데 필수 조건이라는 생각을 반복해서 할 수 밖에 없었다. 상품과 기술력, 서비스만 뛰어나면 글로벌 시장에서 우수한 성과를 보일 수 있을 것 같은데, 정작 매개체 역할을 하는 영어 능력이 부실하면 글로벌 조직문화와 리더십은 요원한 일처럼 느껴지기 때문이다. 마치 한 마을에 울타리를 높게 치고 사는 이웃처럼 연결 역할을 하는 공통 언어가 존재하지 않는다면 역시 한계를 실감할 수밖에 없다.

물론 '영어 대신 한국어는 대체어가 될 수 없는가'라고 생각할 수 있지만 다양한 국가적 배경을 가진 사람들이 대부분 구사하고 있는 언어가 영어라는 측면에서, 또 글로벌 조직문화를 완성하는 측면에서 영어가 가장 빠른 공통 언어로서의 기능을 하는 것도 틀림없어 보인다. 외국인들과 교류하지 않고 한국인들끼리도 잘 하는데……. 라고 생각할 수도 있으나 어차피 우리는 글로벌 시장으로 나아가야 한다는 면에서 우리보다 각국의 시장을 잘 알고 있는 현지인들의 의견을 듣지 않을 수 없다. 그런 측면에서 더욱 다양한 국가의 사람들과 그들의 견해를 수용하는 오픈 마인드는 글로벌 조직문화와 리더십으로 가는 데 반드시 필요하다. 그러므로 영어가 그 시발점이 된다는 것도 인정하지 않을 수 없다. 이제 글로벌 시장에서 성공해야 하는 시대이다. 그럴수록 경쟁의 범위를 넓힐 때 생존 가능성이 높으며, 한국이라는 로컬 특성에 함몰되지 않을 때 성공할 수 있으며, 글로벌 시장에서 작동하지 않는 한국 문화의 병폐를 벗어 던질 때 글로벌 기업으로 인정받게 될 것이다. 이런 이유로 글로벌 기업을 만드는 조직문화와 리더십의 필요성을 다시 한 번 역설하며, 그럼에도 우리가 갖고 있는 자긍심과 강점을 경시하지는 말자는 말 역시 덧붙이고 싶다.

• 자기계발(Self Development) vs 글로벌 자기계발(Global Self Development)

이런 이유로 『The Korea Times』에 기고한 부분을 함께 실었으며 글로벌 마인드, 글로벌 조직문화, 그리고 글로벌 리더십을 발휘하는 창(Window)으로서 독자들이 영어를 활용해 주길 바란다. 지금은 많이 식었지만 한때 자기계발서들이 유행했던 적이 있다. 하지만 이런 환경 때문에 이제 자기계발의 시대를 지나 글로벌 시대의 자기계발 즉, Global Self Development의 방향으로 나아가야 한다고 생각한다. 특히 밀레니얼 세대와 같이 영어 구사력이 뛰어난 사람이 많은 세대뿐만 아니라, 이들에게 리더로서 지원과 코칭을 제공하는 리더들은 Global Self Development에 박차를 가해야 한다고 생각한다. 말하자면 글로벌 기업이 되고자 꿈꾸는 기업이라면 영어는 절대값이다. 당연히 영어 구사력만으로 글로벌 자기계발이 된다고는 생각하지 않는다.

 나아가 이(異)문화의 이해도 함께 힘써야 할 것이다. 한국 이외의 다른 국가 사람들은 어떻게 커뮤니케이션을 하고 관계를 형성하며, 갈등을 해결하고 회의 문화를 가져가는지, 어떻게 상사에게 보고 하고, 또 어떻게 조직 관리를 하는지 등을 이해하고 수용하며 우리의 현재 문화와 접목할 수 있어야 할 것이다. 이런 부분들은 한국의 로컬 문화 또는 한국 기업 문화와 충돌하기 마련인데 이를 극복하는 것은 영어 구사력만으로는 역부족이기 때문이다.

 현재의 로컬 한국 문화를 극복하고 개선하는 데서 나아가 늘 글로벌 수준에 맞는 조직문화와 리더십을 구축하려고 노력을 지속해야 할 것이다. 그런 측면에서 현재 상황을 들여다보는 데 있어 이 책이 일조할 수 있다면 조직 개발이 직업인 나의 미션 일부는 자연스럽게 이루어질 것이라고 본다. 미리 감사의 말씀을 전한다.

3. 조직문화란 무엇인가?

나는 조직문화 진단 및 개선 컨설팅을 업으로 하고 있다. 그러다 보니 자연스럽게 어느 기업을 방문하든 조직문화가 어떠한지를 자세히 보게 된다. 모든 기업의 조직문화가 조금씩 다르다 보니 정형화하여 이런 기업 문화가 가장 좋다고 말하는 것은 당연 어폐가 있다. 또한 전문가들은 조직문화에 좋고 나쁨이 있는 것이 아니라 전략과 성장 방향에 따라 효과적이고 비효과적이라고 이야기한다. 하지만 나는 이 부분에 있어서는 동의하지 않는다. 조직 차원과 기업의 성공에만 초점을 두면 좋은 문화, 나쁜 문화라는 표현이 맞지 않을지 모르지만, 조직 구성원의 측면에서는 좋은 문화가 있고 나쁜 문화가 충분히 있을 수 있기 때문이다. 이 때 중요한 것은 조직 내부의 사람에게만 좋고 나쁨을 논할 수 있는 것이 아니라 조직 외부의 이해 당사자에게도 특정 기업의 문화는 좋게도 작용하고, 나쁘게도 작용할 수 있다는 것이다.

굳이 이 부분을 말하는 것은 조직문화가 좋다는 것은 내외부의 이해 당사자 즉, 직원을 포함하여 그 기업에 관련된 사람들 모두에게 긍정적인 요소가 되기도 하고, 부정적인 요소가 되기도 하기 때문이다. 예를 들어 기업의 고객 서비스에 실망한 고객은 그 기업의 한 직원만 그렇다고 생각하는 것이 아니라, 그 기업 전체의 서비스 문화 수준이 낮다고 생각할 수도 있다. 또 직원들의 업무 몰입 수준이나 조직 만족도는 모두 특정 기업의 문화가 직원들에게 좋고 나쁨으로 충분히 느껴질 수 있음을 나타내기도 한다. 조직의 성장·매출·비즈니스뿐만 아니라 조직 내부 구성원 스스로가 상사에 대해, 스스로의 집단행동에 대해, 그리고 스스로가 조직원들의 인식에 대해 은연중에 느끼는 부분 모두가 평가의 대상, 즉 문화가 된다.

우선 가장 먼저 문화를 이야기할 때 빼놓을 수 없는 것은 눈에 보이는 특정 조직에 독특하게 나타나는 물건들과 상징체계이다. 예를 들어 제조업종에 가면 제조업 특유의 제품을 생산하는 기계들이 존재하기 마련이고, 서비스업종에 가면 서비스업에 맞는 친절과 서비스를 상징하는 물건들이 존재하기 마련이다. 또 식품업종에 가면 그 업종에서 주로 다루는 눈에 띄는 도구들이 있기 마련이다. 이런 부분들은 문화를 상징하는 물체가 된다. 이를 흔히 가공물(Artifact)이라고 부르는데 모든 가공물은 일정 부분 이를 만들어낸 사람들의 정신, 마인드와 연결되어 있다. 예를 들어 건설업계에서 쓰이는 노란 안전모는 건설업종을 나타내지만, 그 본질은 안전을 중시한다는 가치를 담고 있음을 알 수 있다. 그런 면에서 노란 안전모 하나가 그 조직이 무엇을 중시하고 있는지를 상징한다고 할 수 있으며, 이런 가공물들이 기업들이 중시하는 가치와 정열 상태에 놓일 때 기업 내 사람들의 활동은 보다 높은 효과를 거둘 수 있다. 이런 가공물들은 눈으로 보이기 때문에 가장 명확한 수준으로 조직문화를 보여 주는 것 같지만 사실은 그렇지 않다. 눈으로 보이는 가공물과 눈에 보이지 않는 정신이나 마인드셋이 따로 노는 현상, 즉 비정열 상태나 비연결 상태(Culture Disconnect)에 놓일 수 있기 때문에 우리가 가공물만으로 조직문화를 다 읽는다고 하는 것은 무리가 있다.

여기서 하나 주의할 점은 가공물에는 물건이나 상징체계뿐만 아니라 인간의 행동도 포함된다는 것이다. 서비스업 사람들이 보이는 행동과 제조업 사람들이 보이는 행동은 상당히 다르며, 외국계에 있는 사람들과 국내 대기업에 있는 사람들의 행동도 다를 수밖에 없다. 굳이 물건이 아니더라도 행동은 항상 가치를 반영하고 있고, 눈에 보인다는 특성 때문에 가공물로 분류하며, 행동을 관찰해 보면 이 조직에서 무엇이 중요시 되는지를 알 수 있는 상징이 된다. 예를 들어 모 기업에 방문했을 때 전혀 알지 못하는 직원이 화장실에서 이방인인 내게 인사를 했다면 이 조직은 조직이 커서 상호 간에 누구인지 알지 못할 확률이 높지만, 상하관계가 확실하여 자동적으로 자기보다 직급이 높아 보이는 사람에게는 인사를 하는 것이 일상화되어 있다고 추론할 수 있을 것이다. 이처럼 조직 내 사람들이 보이는 행동은 일정한 패턴과 모습을 띠게 되며, 이는 가장 낮은 수준의 문화 요소로서 나타나게 된다. 한 가지 예를 더 든다면 가끔 은행에 근무하는 분들이 가슴에 띠를 두르고 나와서 일렬로 인사를 하는 장면을 목격하게 되는데 이는 은행이라는 업종이 갖는 대고객서비스, 또는 일종의 사내 이벤트성 문화의 일단을 그대로 보여준다고 해도 과언이 아니다.

하지만 이런 가공물은 어디까지나 눈에 보이는 상징 체계여서 유추가 가능하지만, 그 속에 내포하고 있는 깊은 의미와 본질적인 가치를 판단하는 절대적인 기준은 될 수 없다. 특히 행동도 가공물이니 가치를 담고 있을 것이라고 해서 쉽게 그 가치를 판단하고 예측하게 되면 그 조직이 갖고 있는 가치의 본질적인 의미 및 중요성을 오해하거나 간과할 수 있다는 점도 주의할 필요가 있다. 하지만 중요한 것은 모든 가공물은 가치를 일정 부분 반영하고 있음에는 틀림없다는 것이다.

그렇다면 가공물을 만들어내는 가치는 가공물과는 달리 조직문화를 대변하지 못할까? 우리가 흔히 아는 핵심 가치(Core Value)처럼 조직에 장기적으로 중요하고, 모든 조직원들이 소중히 다루어야 할 만큼 조직의 생존에 영향을 미치는 가치는 반드시 눈에 보이는 것은 아니지만 조직문화의 일부로서 크게 작용을 하게 된다. 가치는 가공물보다는 보다 본질적으로 조직문화에 영향을 미치게 되며, 무엇보다 조직 구성원 다수가 신봉하는 신념 체계처럼 의사 결정, 커뮤니케이션, 관계 형성 등에 두루두루 나타나게 된다. '가치'라는 말이 나타내는 것처럼 무엇이 옳고 그른지, 무엇이 중요하고 중요하지 않은지, 무엇이 효과적이고 비효과적인지 등, 일정한 정도 사고와 행동 양식의 방향을 정해주는 역할을 하기 때문에 가공물로 나타나기 이전이라도 조직 내 다수의 사람들에게 영향을 미치고 있는 것이다. 이런 부분에서 조직 내의 중요하고 필수적인 가치를 제대로 정의 내리고 공유하며, 항상 지키려 노력하는 조직과 그렇지 않은 조직은 조직의 효과성 측면에서 차이가 날 수밖에 없다. 그런 면에서 가치는 가공물보다 강력하게 조직문화를 형성하게 되며 집단의 사고와 행동을 결정하는 기준으로서 작용하게 되는 것이다. 따라서 기업이 어떤 가치를 중시하는지를 보면 어떤 문화를 갖고 있는지를 대강 예측할 수 있다.

　　하지만 여기에도 아이러니는 존재한다. 신뢰를 바탕으로 하는 금융 기관이 사내 비리로 쓰러지고, 도전을 중시하는 기업이 혁신 부재로 경쟁에 뒤쳐지며, 가족 같은 기업을 표방하는 기업이 갑질 행태로 대중의 뭇매를 맞는 경우도 비일비재하기 때문이다. 여기에 가치의 역설이 존재하는데, 가치는 항상 말과 글로 쓴다고 해서 반드시 그렇게 나타나지는 않기 때문에 얼마나 내재화하여 나타나는가 하는 점이 무엇보다 중요하다. 또 소비자 건강 제일이라는 가치를 기치로 내세우면서도 안전하지 않은 원료를 쓰는 기업들이 나타나는 것처럼 기업이 비즈니스의 성장에만 초점을 두게 되면 가치와 행동이라는 가공물이 따로 노는 상태, 즉 가치 경시(Value Neglect) 현상도 심심치 않게 나타날 수밖에 없다. 이런 경우 기업에 유익한 가치를 스스로 회피하기 때문에 반드시 장기적으로는 손해를 입을 수밖에 없다. 그래서 가치를 정의 내리고, 공유하고, 내재화하며 지속적으로 환경에 맞게 재정립하는 것은 기업의 성공, 그리고 영속과 떼려야 뗄 수 없는 관계를 맺게 된다.

　　그렇다면 가치는 또 어떻게 만들어질까? 가치의 근원을 따라가게 되면 조직문화의 본질을 보다 깊이 이해할 수 있다. 예를 들어 무사안일주의 문화가 있는 집단의 경우 어떻게 해서 그런 문화 또는 유니크한 집단 현상을 가치로서 수용하게 되었을까? 주목할 것은 이런 집단 행위는 가공물이나 가치처럼 하루아침이나 단기간에 심어서 될 일이 아니다. 오랜 시간 그 조직 내에 존재한 독특한 인자들이 상호 작용을 하여 집단이 이를 자연스럽게 수용하게 만든 과정이 전제되었기에 가능했던 것이다. 그렇다면 집단은 어떻게 특정한 의식을 갖게 되는 것일까? 이에는 여러 가지 이유가 있을 것이다. 보통 그 원인으로 예를 드는 것은 창업주의 철학이나 가치관이다. 창업주가 어떤 사람이었는가, 자기 기업에 대해 어떤 생각을 갖고 있었는가, 그리고 어떤 회사를 만들려고 노력했는가 하는 점은 반드시 그 주변에 있는 사람들에게 영향을 미치며 그것이 가공물과 가치처럼 발현되어 조직 내 자리 잡게 되는 것이다. 여기서 중요한 것은 가공물이나 가치로 발현되는 것보다 훨씬 더 강력하게 집단의 사람들이 당연하게 수용하게 되는 생각, 의식, 판단 이전의 추측들, 무엇은 무엇일 것이라고 상정하는 무의식적 작용들이 결국 조직문화의 원형이라고 부를 수 있다는 점이다.

다소 개념적 설명에 지나지 않는 것처럼 느껴질 수도 있지만, 조직문화의 밑단에는 집단이 받아들이고 습관적으로 수용하는 무의식 차원의 의식이 있다. 이를 흔히 근원적인 집단 가정(Underlying Collective Assumption)이라고 부른다. 이런 집단의 가정 또는 추정은 창업자, 리더, 조직 내 역사, 업종, HR 시스템 등이 기반이 되며 가장 강력하거나 오랜 시간에 걸쳐서 조직의 뿌리처럼 천천히 형성된다. 그런 의미에서 조직문화를 바꾼다는 것은 집단이 무의식 차원에서 본질적으로 받아들이고 있는 이런 집단 가정을 흔들어 새롭게 정비할 수 있을 때에만 가능한 것이다. 이런 이유로 조직문화 변화는 문화를 형성한 시간만큼은 아니더라도 오랜 시간이 걸리는 과정이며, 집단과 개인의 마인드를 리셋하는 것처럼 상당한 노력도 함께 기울일 때 가능한 것이다. 말하자면 행동을 포함하는 가공물과 가치를 발현시키는 더 깊은 심연의 무의식인 집단 가정은 뿌리 깊은 조직문화의 실체가 된다고 해도 과언이 아니다.

예를 들어 기업을 방문하면 부서 간 분열과 목표 의식 저조, 지나친 경직성과 서열화, 너무 잦은 변화가 혼란의 원인이 된다. 그리고 이는 문화로서 인식되어 사람들은 그 체제 자체를 바꾸는 것이 힘들다고 느끼며, 이 조직은 원래 그런 조직이라고 당연시하게 되는데 이는 벌써 집단의 가정이 그렇게 경직화되어 있음을 나타낸다. 그러다보니 껍질을 깨듯 새로운 변화를 추구하는 것은 힘들다는 것에 모두가 이미 무의식적으로 동의하고 있음을 나타낸다. 뿐만 아니라 우리 조직은 응당 그런 곳이려니 하고 받아들이게 되니 그런 문화 기조는 계속해서 고착되고, 새로운 문화는 찾아오기 힘들게 된다. 이는 바로 근원적 집단 가정을 어떻게 만들어내는가가 조직문화의 핵심이 된다는 것을 설명해 준다.

이렇게 조직문화는 다양한 층위와 복잡한 요소들로 만들어지는데, 조직문화의 개선 방향도 이를 전반적으로 가미하여 추구되어야 하며, 모든 요소들이 상호 작용을 하고 있다는 점을 간과해서는 안된다. 근원적 집단 가정은 가치를 낳고, 가치는 행동을 포함한 가공물을 낳으며, 역으로 가공물은 가치에, 가치는 다시 근원적 집단 가정에 영향을 미치게 되는 것이다. 뿐만 아니라 조직이 갖고 있는 경쟁 환경, 기술 수준, 재무적 수준, 인사 정책 등 비인적 요소들도 문화에 간섭을 하게 되는데 이런 요소들이 미치는 영향도 절대 간과할 수 없다. 그런데 여기서 조직 구조, 경쟁, 업계 현황, 상품과 서비스 등이 단순할수록 인적 자원의 영향은 절대적이라 할 수 있다. 특히 창업자를 포함한 최고 경영진과 관리자들은 조직문화를 고착시키기도 하고 희석시키기도 하는데, 그들이 집단 가정 형성에 가장 큰 목소리를 내고, 가치를 발현하는 것을 찬성하거나 금지시키게 하며, 또 가공물을 만들어내는 권한을 갖기 때문이다. 또 좋은 기업 문화일수록 리더들이 이런 여러 층위의 조직문화 요소들을 몸으로 실천하고 있다는 측면에서 롤 모델링(Role Modeling)을 수행한다는 점도 빼놓을 수 없다고 할 수 있다. 물은 위에서 아래로 흐르며, 윗물이 맑아야 아랫물이 맑다는 말처럼 문화도 위에서 아래로 흐른다는 점은 사람이 만드는 조직에서는 너무나 당연한 이야기일 것이다.

4. 글로벌 기업을 만드는 조직문화와 리더십

그렇다면 이 책에서 이야기하려고 하는 글로벌 기업을 만드는 조직문화와 리더십으로의 변화는 어떻게 추진해야 할까? 우리는 무엇보다 문화의 변화를 추구하는 사람, 특히 문화 형성에 지대한 영향을 미치는 리더들을 중심으로 변화해야 한다는 점에 대해서는 말하지 않아도 컨센서스를 형성하고 있다. 그렇다면 어떤 방식으로 문화 변화를 가져가는 것이 가장 바람직할까? 지금까지의 경험으로는 글로벌 기업 문화와 글로벌 리더십에 초점을 두는 것이 지극히 효과적이고 최종의 도전이라고 생각한다. 최근 몇 년간 불어온 수평적 조직문화와 리더십의 트렌드도 이를 반영하고 있다.

그렇다면 글로벌 조직문화와 리더십은 어떤 특징을 갖고 있을까? 다양한 국가에서 온 사람들과 워크숍을 진행할 때마다 특정 기업의 문화가 어떤 면에서 글로벌 조직문화에서 벗어나 있는지, 어떤 측면에서 글로벌 리더십을 보다 갖추어야 할지를 여실히 느낄 수 있었다. 문화는 상대적이기 때문에 어느 문화가 좋거나 나쁘다고 할 수 없다고 이야기해 왔지만, 수직적인 문화보다는 수평적인 문화로의 이행이 대세가 되고 있는 것처럼 문화는 발전 단계가 있다고 생각되는 것도 부인할 수 없다. 또 이는 글로벌 전문가들의 의견이기도 하다.

첫째, 글로벌 기업 문화와 리더십으로의 변화를 추구하고자 한다면 수직보다는 수평이 문제가 적고, 바람직하다고 생각하는 것이 일반적이다. 한국의 기업들이 갖고 있는 병폐와 폐단으로서 수직적인 문화를 고쳐야 한다고 생각하는 외국인 임직원들과 대화를 하다 보면 글로벌 기업으로서의 위상 정립에 기업 문화가 갖는 수직성과 경직성은 분명 역작용을 하고 있다는 것이 명확하기 때문이다. 이직율과 조직 몰입도에 심대한 영향을 미치며, 한국 기업 문화에 대한 평가를 할 때도 반드시 지적되는 요소이기도 하다. 나는 지난 한 해에도 천여 명의 외국인 임직원들에게 정기적인 일대일 임원 코칭 및 워크숍을 제공한 경험이 있는데 이때 거론되는 단골 메뉴가 바로 수직적인 조직문화와 리더십이었다. 그렇다면 이런 수직성을 수평적 문화로 변화시키지 않고 글로벌 조직문화와 리더십을 발휘할 수 있을까? 물론 응당 불가능하다고 생각한다.

둘째, 집단적인 문화보다는 개인적인 문화가 글로벌 문화에 가깝다고 생각하는 것도 두드러지는 특성 중 하나이다. 이 부분은 서열이 높은 리더를 중심으로 행동하는 수직성과도 일정 부분 연관이 있는데, 다양한 국가 출신의 사람들이 이야기하는 한국 문화의 일면 중 하나가 개인의 다름을 쉽게 인정하지 않는다는 것이다. 그룹이 내는 의견에 동조하는 것을 미덕으로 알고, 그룹에 승인을 받을 수 있을 때에만 개인의 의견이 건전하고 유익한 것으로 판단하는 성향 역시 글로벌 기업으로 가는 조직문화와 리더십의 측면에서는 마이너스 요인인 것이다. 예를 들어 인터뷰를 위해 만난 한 유럽 출신 임원은 회의에 들어갈 때마다 한국인들이 단체로 이야기를 하지 않는 모습을 자주 보는데, 어떤 면에서는 리더의 생각이 보다 중요하다고 가정하는 측면과 개인의 의견은 집단이나 조직 의견보다 항상 덜 중요하다는 측면 때문인 것 같다고 나름 풀이를 했다. 문제는 글로벌이라는 시각에서 볼 때 다름과 개인의 고유성을 인정하지 못하면 창의적 문제 해결에 장애가 되고, 조직문화는 보다 경직될 수밖에 없으며, 단일화되고 오픈되지 못한다는 특성이 작용할 것이다. 글로벌 기업 문화를 떠올리면 이와는 정반대의 속성, 예를 들어 다양성, 다채로움, 그리고 오픈 마인드를 요구하기 때문에 개인의 자유와 의사를 수용할 필요가 다분하다고 할 수 있다.

이는 단순히 개인과 조직의 측면만을 의미하지 않는다. 상당히 많은 외국 출신의 임직원들은 한국 기업에서 일하면서 전문가가 드물고, 책임을 지려는 사람이 드물다는 점에 놀라곤 한다. 이는 한국의 기업 문화 자체가 리더들의 의견을 지나치게 중요시하고, 내부적인 논의를 거쳐야만 결정을 할 수 있는 풍토 때문이라고 생각한다. 그러다 보니 설령 업무를 담당하는 사람이라도 권한을 행사하거나 역할을 수행하기 힘들며, 독자적이기보다는 문제가 되지 않는 수준의 행동과 의사 결정을 하게 되는 것이다. 결론적으로 이는 다시 조직문화적 병폐가 되어 기업의 성장을 가로막는 요소로 작용하게 된다. 또 전문가로서 행동할 수 있는 사람들을 만나지 못하게 되는 것이다. 어떻게 담당자로 10년을 일해도 독자적인 의사 결정을 할 수 없을까? 그러다 보니 외국인들의 눈에는 전문가가 없는 것으로 보일 수 있는 것이다. 나아가 창의성이 떨어지고, 성과 중심 문화가 저해되고, 권한 위임이 전혀 되지 않는 현상도 생기는 것이다. 한국 기업의 임직원들을 상대해본 외국인 임직원 중에는 이런 집단주의 성향의 병폐에 대해 호소하는 사람들이 제법 많았다. 물론 기성세대의 입장에서는 밀레니얼 세대의 개인주의 성향을 질타하는 분들도 있지만, 이는 세계적 문화 조류의 일부이며, 글로벌 기업 문화를 추구하는 입장에서는 거쳐갈 수밖에 없는 흐름이라는 점도 참고하자.

마지막으로, 다른 하나의 조직문화적 변화 방향을 이야기한다면, 조직이 중요한가 개인의 삶이 중요한가 하는 점이다. 회사를 개인의 삶과 엄격히 분리하여 조직의 일을 하러 오는 곳으로 생각하는 우리의 풍토는 특히 서구권의 임직원들과 이야기를 하면 제법 큰 차이를 나타낸다. 예를 들어 출근 시간에 조금 늦었다고 주의와 경고를 주는 한국인 팀장을 이해할 수 없는 외국인 임직원이 많은데, 그들은 가정사에 중요한 일들이 있다면 늦게 올 수도 있으며, 늦게 온 만큼 늦게 가면 문제가 될 것이 없지 않느냐고 항변한다. 예를 들어 아이가 유치

원에서 행사를 하거나 갑자기 아파서 등, 여러 가지 측면에서 가정에는 일이 있을 수밖에 없는데 그런 일을 조금도 이해하지 못하는 것은 조직을 너무 삭막한 공간으로 만드는 것이 아니냐고 이야기한다. 나아가 업무 시간의 양만을 따지는 것이 아니라 단위 시간 내 업무량이나 집중도를 생각한다면 업무 시간에 조금 늦는 점을 문제 삼을 것은 크게 없지 않느냐고 반문하는 외국인들을 제법 많이 보았다.

이 또한 글로벌 기업으로 가는 하나의 관문이라고 생각하는데, 근로자 복지 수준을 넘어서 직원들의 개인의 삶이 업무에 큰 지장을 주거나 피해를 주는 것이 아니라면 수용할 수 있는 문화를 만드는 것도 매우 중요한 측면으로 생각된다. 우리나라도 과거에 조직에 몰입하고 함몰되는 임직원들의 역량을 높이 사던 분위기에서 요즘에는 일과 삶의 균형을 추구하는 쪽으로 많이 바뀌고 있는데, 이는 앞으로 더욱 중요한 몫으로 기업 문화적 측면에서 변화가 올 수 있다고 생각한다.

물론 비단 이런 예 만으로 글로벌 기업 문화와 리더십을 확정하거나 아니면 그것이 최선인 양 말할 수는 없을 것이다. 하지만 그럼에도 많은 외국의 임직원들이 힘들어하고 있고, 선진국들의 패턴이 이를 따라갔다는 점만으로도 보다 경제와 문화의 선진화를 추구하는 우리 사회와 기업들에게는 참고할 점이 된다고 생각한다. 또 이를 선도하거나 만드는 역할을 하는 리더들은 바람직한 변화라는 관점에서 어느 정도 자기 견해를 가질 필요도 존재할 것이다. 그런 면에서 이 책이 작으나마 도움이 되길 기대한다.

5. 조직문화의 변화는 가능한가?

사실 변화는 항상 내부의 의지보다는 외부의 필요에 의해서 더욱 많이 발생한다. 즉 변화는 필요에 의해서 가장 확실하게 발생하며, 당위가 없거나 필요를 만들어내지 못하면 실패할 수밖에 없는 것이 숙명이기도 하다. 조직문화의 변화 역시 이와 다르지 않아서, 현황에 대한 인식과 성찰이 없이는 요원한 일이다. 그러다 보니 외부 환경의 변화를 어떻게 인식하고 대응할 것인가 하는 점은 무엇보다 중요하다. 많은 기업들이 성과의 측면에서, 밀레니얼과 같은 새로운 조직 구성원의 측면에서 조직문화의 변화를 꾀하려고 노력한다. 이는 좀 더 확대해보면 생존, 성장, 그리고 성공의 측면에서 기업들이 조직문화의 중요성을 크게 인식하고 있다는 것을 의미한다. 관련하여 수많은 학자들과 전문가들이 조직문화가 실제 조직의 성과에 30% 이상 차이를 가져온다고 지적하는 부분은 다시 거론할 필요도 없을 것이다.

다만 문제는 조직문화 변화의 프로세스를 세심히 준비하는 것, 전 임직원이 참여하여 근원적 집단 가정을 뒤집는 것, 그리고 그런 작업을 무리하고 지루하지 않게 하기 위해서 소위 말하는 작은 목표(Small Wins)를 만들어내는 것 등, 시간을 갖고 준비하고 점검해야 할 요소들이 많다는 점이 늘 변화에 걸림돌이 된다. 말하자면 이벤트가 아닌 항시 업무가 되어, 단기적인 결실을 맺는 것에 초점을 두는 것이 아니라 새로운 비즈니스 패러다임에 맞는 새로운 집단 사고의 틀(Thinking Frame)을 형성하려는 노력을 할 수 있을 때 문화 변화는 충실히 이행될 수 있을 것이다. 그리고 그때에만 조직의 성장과 성공으로 문화가 견인 역할을 할 수 있을 것이다. 끝으로 어떤 노력을 하던 문화를 변화시킨다는 것은 집단 가정의 틀 전체를 바꾸는 것으로서 소수가 아닌 다수, 개인의 문제가 아닌 조직 차원의 노력이어야 한다는 점에도 주의를 기울여야 한다. 그런 면에서 다양한 조직 구성원을 변화에 최대로 참여시키는 노력, 이른바 믹스맥스(Mixmax) 방식은 어떤 측면에서는 의미가 크다.

6. 조직문화와 리더십을 보는 관점

조직 내 리더들은 조직문화와 리더십에 대해 자신의 관점을 형성하고 있어야 한다. 조직문화를 어떻게 파악하고 개선하며, 변화시켜가야 하는지, 리더십 역시 이러한 관점에서 지속적인 변화 노력을 할 수 있어야 한다. 업무가 바쁨에도 이런 노력을 해야 하는 것은 고성과 문화를 만드는 밑바탕이 조직문화와 리더십에 있기 때문이다. 그런 면에서 리더들이 참고해야 할 점들은 다음과 같을 것이다.

조직 내 리더들이 범하기 쉬운 실수 중 하나는 조직 전체의 입장을 감안하지 않는다는 것이다. 자신이 속한 팀, 자신이 속한 부서, 그리고 자신이 속한 본부의 이익과 관심에 함몰되거나 심지어 자신의 이익에 집중하게 된다는 것이다. 하지만 기업 내 임직원의 존재 이유는 조직 전체의 이익을 극대화하는 데 있기 때문에 조직 전체의 입장을 감안하려는 노력을 하지 않는 것은 어떤 의미에서는 조직 효과성 파괴에 가깝다. 물론 조직 내 시스템이 어떻게 작동하고 있는가에 따라 개인이 할 수 있는 범위는 극히 제한될 수밖에 없다. 하지만 제한된 범위를 넘어 조직 전체의 입장과 관심을 따라 움직여야 하는 것이 리더의 바람직한 태도임에도 틀림이 없다. 이에 반하는 욕구를 떨쳐 버릴 수 있을 때 조직문화와 리더십은 보다 건강해지고, 조직은 보다 큰 성공을 거둘 수 있다.

　그런 면에서 조직 내 리더의 활동은 모두 전략과 매칭될 필요성이 있다. 우리가 리더십이라는 스킬 차원의 행위에 지나치게 관심을 갖고 조직문화가 좋다/나쁘다는 가치 평가에 집중하기 때문에, 리더들은 업무를 제대로 해나가지 못하고 종종 조직 내 다양한 사람들의 눈치를 본다. 그러다 보니 제대로 된 리더십과 조직문화 형성을 하지도 못한 채 전략 이행의 행위마저 제한을 받는 경우가 왕왕 있다. 하지만 위에서 말했듯 조직 내 리더들은 조직을 위해서 일해야 하는 것처럼 전략을 위해 일해야 하는 것도 틀림이 없다. 전략을 위해 일할 때만이 성과를 효과적으로 관리할 수 있고, 이에 필요한 리더십을 설정할 수 있으며, 나아가 고성과 조직문화를 형성할 수 있다. 우리가 문화라는 개념에 과도하게 휩싸여 있는 동안 글로벌 경쟁사들은 끊임없이 전략을 새롭게 하고 경쟁의 파도를 밀고 오고 있다는 점도 간과해서는 안 된다. 말하자면 리더십과 조직문화의 개선 행동은 지속하되 전략 추구에도 지속적으로 중점할 때, 리더십과 조직문화는 보다 성과 중심으로 개편될 수 있다. 그런 면에서 조직문화와 함께 전략 추구라는 큰 방향을 항상 함께 염두해 두면 좋을 것이다. 특히 이런 현상은 작금에 조직문화 개선을 강조하는 기업들이 많이 나오면서 리더들이 생각해 보아야 할 현상인데, 문화 정화 때문에 전략 추구를 소홀히 할 수는 없다는 점을 다시 한번 지적하고자 한다.

　추가적으로, 갈수록 많은 조직들이 일회성 리더십 스킬을 교육하면서 중장기적으로 중점해야 하는 역량에는 큰 관심을 쏟지 않는 추세이다. 이는 글로벌 트렌드도 마찬가지인데, 예측할 수 없이 빠른 비즈니스 환경 변화 때문이라고 생각된다. 하지만 리더들의 임무가 조직을 위해 일하는 것이고, 전략을 추구하는 것이라면 이에 필요한 근육, 즉 역량을 길러내는 것은 망각되어서는 안될 근원적인 미션이다. 리더십의 발휘도 이와 다르지 않아서 업계 경쟁이 요구하는 역량, 고성과 리더가 함양해야 하는 역량, 업무 프로세스가 요구하는 역량을 끊임없이 추구하고 개발하여야 한다. 또 이 모든 것들은 결국 전략 추구라는 큰 줄기에서 뻗어져 나오는 것이 가장 바람직하다. 이를 위해서 조직 내 리더들은 업계 내 조직의 발전 방향에 대해 관심을 멈추지 말아야 하며, 뛰어난 리더가 어떻게 성과를 내는가에 대해서 지속적인 관심을 가져야 하고, 앞으로 비즈니스는 어떤 변화를 거쳐갈 것인가에 대해서 고심을 지속해야 한다. 결국 뛰어난 리더십과 조직문화를 만드는 조직은 역량이라는 무기를 탑재하고 있다는 사실을 잊어서는 안 된다. 역량이 제대로 숨 쉴 수 있는 환경을 만들면 이 또한 건강한 조직문화가 된다. 나아가 조직 차원의 역량 확보가 결국은 권한 위임의 조직문화로, 학습이 가능한 조직문화로, 또 고객 중심의 변화가 가능한 조직으로 성장하는 길임을 잊지 말자.

마지막으로 업종의 타깃을 글로벌 기업에 두자. 지난 수십 년간 한국의 성장은 우리로 하여금 자긍심과 자신감을 충분히 갖게 만들었다. 그런 면에서는 우리 스스로 자랑스러움을 가져도 좋지만 우리가 하는 경쟁은 앞으로 모두 글로벌 경쟁이다. 그런데 글로벌 경쟁을 위주로 하려면 글로벌 시장에서 뛰어난 마켓 플레이어들과 겨루어야 하는데 우리는 양적 성장은 많은 부분 집적했지만, 질적 성장에서는 아직도 갈 길이 먼 부분이 많이 있다. 이른바 시스템 차원인데, 업종별로 100년 이상의 역사를 갖고 있는 서구 선진 국가들을 우리가 지난 몇십 년간 성장했다고 해서 모두 따라잡았다고 생각하는 것은 큰 착각에 다름없다. 바로 이 측면이 앞으로 우리가 가장 고민해야 하는 측면 중 하나로, 일하는 방식, 프로세스, 상호 부서 간의 유기적 조합 등 시스템 차원에서 어떻게 움직일 때 가장 시너지가 크고 성과가 최대화될 수 있는지 지금보다 훨씬 지대한 관심을 가져야 한다. 상품이, 마케팅이, 그리고 기술이 부분으로서 작용하는 것이 아니라 이 전체가 하나의 시스템으로 작동하게 되면 보다 큰 성과를 창출할 수 있을터이니 말이다. 한국에 부임해 오는 수많은 외국인 임직원들이 말하는 부분 역시 바로 시스템이다. 부분의 기술은 뛰어나고, 인적 자원이 뛰어날지라도 오랜 시간 시스템 차원의 업무 방식을 구축한 기업들을 넘어서는 것은 그렇게 쉬운 일이 아니다. 시스템이 리더십과 조직문화 차원으로 연결될 때 보다 큰 상승효과를 가져온다는 점을 조직 내 리더들은 잊지 말아야 한다. 즉, 글로벌 시장에서의 경쟁력을 시스템을 근간으로 구축한 기업들을 참고하며, 우리의 시스템을 하루빨리 구축해 나가야 한다. 높은 수준의 시스템은 높은 수준의 인재 문화(Talents Culture)를 반영하고 있다는 점도 우리가 유념해 보아야 할 부분이다. 이런 노력 속에서 조직문화와 리더십이 보다 글로벌 마켓 리더의 그것으로 발전해 갈 수 있을 것이다. 앞으로는 시스템으로 승부하는 글로벌 기업들을 타깃으로 뛸 준비를 해야 한다.

7. 이 책의 활용 방안

1) 임원 및 팀장 워크숍/코칭

이 책은 대중들을 위해서 쓴 것이 아니라 조직 내 리더와 관리자들, 임원진들이 글로벌 자기계발을 함께 하며 조직 내 문제와 이슈를 인식하고, 특히 리더십과 조직문화 차원에서 접근할 수 있기를 바라서 쓴 것이다. 그런 면에서 워크숍이나 코칭을 통해 그 효과를 극대화할 수 있다고 생각한다. 이 책에 실린 『The Korea Times』에 쓴 기사들을 통해 자신의 의견과 견주어 보고 찬반 양면을 살펴보며, 조직에 대한 관점을 강화하고, 스스로 자문해볼 수 있으면 좋을 것이다. 조직 내 문제와 이슈를 해결해야 하는 리더의 입장에서 무엇이 문제인가를 찾는 것은 지극히 필요한 행위이며, 이 책이 기여할 수 있다면 큰 감사를 표하고 싶다.

2) 조직문화 개선 워크숍/코칭

많은 조직들이 리더십과 조직문화 개선을 개개인의 리더와 관리자 책임으로 부여한다. 하지만 조직 내에는 공통된 인식과 접근을 요하는 경우가 많으며, 이를 위해서는 그룹으로 활동하는 것이 보다 양질의 결과를 가져오는 경우도 많다. 특히 조직 내 리더들이 조직 역량 차원에서 생각해 보아야 할 이슈나 조직문화 개선처럼 집단의 가정을 터치해 주어야 하는 경우에는 더더욱 그러하다. 이 책이 그런 면에서 기여할 수 있기를 바라는데, 리더십과 조직문화는 개인 차원이 아닌 조직 차원, 그룹의 관점과 행동으로 이어질 때 보다 양질의 결과를 가져올 수 있다는 점에서 그러하다. 말하자면 리더십과 조직문화의 패턴과 양상이 그룹 차원으로 나타난다는 점에서도 개선 노력을 공통으로 해 나가는 것도 하나의 방법이라고 생각한다. 조직에 대해 생각해볼 중요 이슈와 문제들에 대해서 관심을 갖고 스스로 질문에 답할 수 있을 때 리더십과 조직문화는 그 힘을 입증할 수 있을 것이라고 생각한다.

3) 영어 그룹 코칭 및 강의 워크북

지금까지 수많은 글로벌 기업의 사람들을 만나면서 갖게 된 생각 중 하나는 우리 스스로 자신감을 충분히 가져도 좋을 만큼 한국은 이미 성장해 있다는 것이다. 개별 상품과 서비스의 수준에서는 글로벌 수준에 충분히 도달했기 때문에 이를 바탕으로 경쟁해도 무방하리라고 생각한다. 하지만 우리 기업들이 보다 글로벌 차원에서 일진보하고, 글로벌 효과성을 최대로 발휘하기 위해서는 아직도 개선해야 할 리더십과 조직문화의 양상들이 많이 존재하는 것 또한 사실이다. 그런 면에서 모든 리더와 관리자들은 개인적인 계발 노력을 경주할 필요가 있으며, 개인 별로 성찰과 다짐의 시간을 자주 가질 필요가 있다고 생각한다. 하루아침에 리더십과 조직문화가 개선되는 것이 아니므로 기존에 갖고 있던 생각들을 정리하고, 타파하며, 새로운 관점을 수용하기 위한 노력도 경주해야 한다고 생각한다. 이를 반영할 경우 그룹 토론은 충분히 유익한 대안이 될 수 있으며 이 경우 각 챕터마다 포함되어 있는 찬/반 의견을 정리하여 토론을 해보는 것도 좋은 시도가 될 것이라고 생각한다. 이를 영어 그룹 코칭/워크숍으로 시도하는 것도 조직 내 새로운 학습의 형태가 될 수 있을 것이라고 생각한다. 직급에 무관하게 많은 기업의 임직원들이 이미 어떤 형태로든 영어 공부를 하고 있으므로, 글로벌 시대의 자기계발, 이제 영어로 하는 강의 등의 학습을 자연스럽게 받아들이자.

II

글로벌 기업을 만드는
리더십

Leadership

1. 리더십 철학 갖기 Leadership Philosophy

Leadership Insights : 대부분의 경우 리더십을 스킬로서 교육하고 개발하려고 노력합니다. 하지만 리더들이 자신의 역할과 책임에 대해 강한 의식을 갖는 철학적인 성찰이 없으면, 리더십 스킬은 무용지물에 다르지 않습니다.

As a leadership facilitator, I visit a lot of companies that are interested in creating their own training programs. Every spring in particular, many organizations show a keen interest in how to grow leadership in their organizations. Because everyone knows the importance of leadership and its effect on an organization, most organizations are primarily concerned with the end results of their leadership programs. However, more important than the specific form of the program which, after all, might be identical to that of other organizations' programs is an organization's leadership philosophy. A leadership philosophy is the essence of a leadership program, and it should be created, shared and internalized before the program is even designed.

Many thriving companies have their own leadership development programs to which their success is often attributed. Nevertheless, many HR professionals in Korea think that their leadership development programs are similar or very similar to those of other industry-leading companies. One HR professional that I know even commented that although his company has a well-structured and beautifully-designed leadership program, there is no philosophy that lays down the foundation of what's important to the company, why it's important, and any implicit messages that accompany these values.

How often have you witnessed excellent leadership? For what reason do you think having excellent leadership is so crucial to your organization? I am asking these questions because a lot of leaders in organizations still demonstrate a lot of problems in spite of numerous training and coaching programs. I also would like to ask why it is so difficult for a corporation to become a financially sustainable company if their leadership development programs are delivered successfully. I think that the answer to these sorts of questions lies in corporations not teaching leadership philosophy and simply teaching leadership skills to manage personnel more effectively and efficiently. Expanding further, can an organization without a philosophy exist perpetually? No, it can't. Neither can a leader and it is a leader's role to create a sustainable company whose goals extend beyond short-term financial performance.

In this context, there are several questions that should be posed to leaders before they participate and learn about leadership and its skills. What is important in your behavior as a leader and why? What are the guiding principles of your behaviors and from where do those behavioral principles derive? What meanings do your principles and beliefs that you have as a leader give to yourself, your employees, your department, and your organization? How important do you believe your leadership philosophy is, how important does your organization believe it is, and what impact do you believe it will bring to your organization? These questions are essential because what you believe should be the same as what you say and how you behave. If they are inconsistent, the misalignment between belief and behaviors will weaken your leadership and bring confusion about what is true and what is not true in your organization. This will eventually reduce the probability of your company's sustainability.

Nowadays, many Korean organizations have a desire to become more agile and responsive to market changes. However, if their managers have weak and wavering philosophies about leadership, this will inevitably show itself in their actions, which means they cannot maintain consistency. In addition, leadership philosophies are crucial because they contain ethics and values that are the core elements of leaders' behavior. Most organizations already emphasize the importance of their mission, vision and values as well as value-based behaviors; a leadership philosophy is a natural extension of this.

Leadership is different from management, and should bring bigger value to organizations than mere financial performance. This is the season in which many HR professionals begin thinking about what leadership trainings should be implemented in their organizations. Given this, I hope they do not forget that many leaders with great leadership skills end up leaving organizations due to ethical issues. What are the responsibilities and duties your leaders should perform in any corporate situation?

질문 1 조직 현황을 돌아볼 때 여러분 조직을 효과적으로 이끌기 위해서는 어떤 리더십이 필요하다고 생각하십니까?

질문 2 여러분이 조직의 리더로서 갖고 있는 자신의 행동 기반이 되는 철학은 무엇입니까?

질문 3 여러분 조직 내 리더들의 윤리 지수는 어떻다고 생각하십니까?

본 아티클에 대해 여러분은 개인적으로 찬성하십니까? 아니면 반대하십니까? 그 근거는 무엇입니까? (찬반 토론도 주제를 이해하는 좋은 방법입니다.)

Pros(찬)	Cons(반)
✔	✔
✔	✔
✔	✔
✔	✔
✔	✔

- 본 주제에 대한 여러분의 최종 의견은 무엇입니까?

2. 참된 리더십 True Leadership

Leadership Insights : 리더로서 강점이 많을수록 뛰어난 리더가 된다고 생각하기 쉽지만, 진정한 리더가 된다는 것은 어떤 면에서는 자신의 나약한 모습을 직면할 수 있을 때 시작됩니다.

Holding a high position in an organization is not enough to ensure that someone is viewed as a true leader. It's not that people don't respect that person's position; rather, it's that a genuine connection between the employee and the leader needs to exist before the employee will acknowledge that person as their "leader" in the truest sense of the word. If this connection is missing, then the "leader" will be a leader on the surface alone; a leader whose leadership will always be in doubt. This can move employees to become more disengaged from their organizations and their work. Thus, becoming a true leader is very important to an organization's development.

In order to compete globally, many Korean companies have recently begun to change their corporate structure, positional hierarchy, and corporate culture in order to create a horizontal culture in which their employees are voluntarily more participative and productive. The success of these companies is due, in part, to the enhancement of their leaders' leadership and communication skills, and the creation of a positive organizational atmosphere. However, what really matters, and what is rarely discussed, is that none of these things are possible unless leaders are prepared to be emotionally connected to their employees.

How, then, do leaders develop this "true leadership?" Theoretically, it's simple enough. In practice, however, it requires great courage: you must unflinchingly and frankly assess yourself. If leaders become aware of their own painful misbehavior and weaknesses, followers will begin admiring and respecting them for it, according to Daniel Goleman, a professor at Harvard Business School. Goleman emphasizes that being honest with yourself and with others are the trademark characteristics of self-aware leaders.

Let me use a real example. I had the opportunity to coach a senior executive who worked for a large multinational company. When I began the coaching engagement, I conducted a 360 degree feedback review for him, for which I interviewed his 23 colleagues. These 23 people said almost exactly the same things about this leader's weaknesses in response to questions about his areas for improvement. When I met the coach face to face and gave him the feedback results, he became very defensive, claiming that he knew exactly who had said what and arguing that such-and-such person was not qualified to say that. The leader hated what he heard, and insisted that this portrait was "not the true him." For the next several months, he was reluctant to cooperate with me because he was not ready to admit that the person that his colleagues had described was his true self.

He did not know how authoritative he was, how much he was stopping other colleagues from being autonomous and participative, and how big a hindrance he was to creating a desirable organizational culture. It was hard for him to admit that others saw him differently than he saw himself. Since his lack of self-knowledge did not allow him to connect with other people, he was not a true leader, but merely a fake leader who only micromanaged his followers.

After about three months, when we were in the middle of the coaching engagement, he began to change his attitude and tried to transform himself a bit more actively. However, unfortunately, he did not change as much as his followers and boss had hoped. Can you guess what happed to him? He remained a leader without any authentic power to move people, and without a true connection to his followers. Did he ever achieve true power, authority and influence as a leader? Unfortunately, not. He chose to remain a fake leader due to his refusal to truly connect to his followers by developing self-awareness.

To admit as a leader what your own leadership looks like is a tough task. It is not easy to get rid of the notion that admitting your mistakes will make you weaker. However, what really makes you weak is not changing what other people think you need to change. As Cornell University's 2012 research proved, self-awareness is a critical trait of successful leaders. Once they admit their flaws and weaknesses, organizations can become participative spaces where employees can open their hearts and talk freely. Leaders need to adapt to the times in order to remain effective. The leadership models and traits needed today are different from what was needed traditionally. That is why leaders must find the courage to accept how others view them.

질문 4 조직 내에서 여러분은 어느 정도 리더로서 참된 존경을 받고 있습니까?

질문 5 스스로가 생각하는 자신의 이미지와, 동료들이 리더로서 생각하는 여러분의 이미지는 얼마나 일치합니까?

질문 6 리더로서 갖고 있는 강점이 제대로 발휘되기 위해서는 스스로에게 어떤 변화가 필요하다고 생각하십니까?

본 아티클에 대해 여러분은 개인적으로 찬성하십니까? 아니면 반대하십니까? 그 근거는 무엇입니까?

Pros(찬)	Cons(반)
✔	✔
✔	✔
✔	✔
✔	✔
✔	✔

- 본 주제에 대한 여러분의 최종 의견은 무엇입니까?

3. 리더십 계발하기 Training vs. Growing Leaders

Leadership Insights : 조직의 미래를 위해 필요한 리더를 기르는 것은 당장의 수익을 내는 것 이상으로 중요합니다. 그런 면에서 차세대 리더를 어떤 방식과 전략에 근거하여 양성해야 할 것인지는 모든 현장 리더들이 함께 생각해보아야 할 과제입니다.

I have been leading study groups of around 20-30 HR professionals from large Korean companies since 2017. This year, we have started to concentrate on how to create a leadership development program. Here are some of the points that have come up.

1) Traditional or not

Corporations should decide whether they will create a leadership development program for themselves or not. Then they also need to decide the program's methodology: how they will develop their future leaders. Most companies don't give very much thought to this latter consideration: when I surveyed participants about whether their leadership development program included any other methods besides a traditional training, more than 80 percent of HR professionals answered no. This, in and of itself, is not necessarily a problem, as the uniqueness of a leadership development program matters less than its effectiveness. However, my concern is that companies stick with traditional methods without having thought enough about whether these methods are the best fit for them. We need to ask ourselves: Which methods will help most? Is leaders' growth hindered by a traditional frame? Can we choose a development method after we decide what sort of growth leaders need? Efforts to develop leaders successfully should start without any predetermined method; the methodology should be selected only after the direction and the content have already been decided on. This is the converse of what is currently happening.

2) Organizations vs. individuals

One downside of leadership development in Korean corporations is that it is typically used to resolve flaws and problems that many leaders have. However, without an organization-wide clear definition of, and approach to, collective leadership, these attempts will remain as tools used only to improve individual leaders, which is a mistake, as they could be doing so much more to help the organization overall. Leadership development can develop the organization as a whole by developing leaders organization-wide; this requires leaders to have a clear vision for where the organization is going and to know what competencies are strategically needed. Using leadership development to solve issues, then, is actually backward, as competencies will be thought about first (as goals in and of themselves) as opposed to second (as tools). True leadership development lies in developing leaders who will lead an organization, not in solving people's specific problems. They are correlated, but they are different. Overcome the temptation to fix currently-visible problems and instead look forward to developing the organization.

3) Strategy vs. culture

Leadership development is ultimately about how to grow people. However, figuring out in which direction to grow people is also a major problem. Since the final goal of for-profit corporations is to achieve financial prosperity, you might think the direction would be self-apparent, but the reality is different. I am not in any way lessening the importance of organizational culture; however, HR professionals tend to focus too much on culture when they work on leadership development. They forget that the most important thing for leadership development to achieve is to bring the corporation further in line with its overall strategy and business blueprint. Culture is a direct reflection of the past and present of an organization, but strategy is its future; therefore, prioritizing culture over strategy is not keeping the bigger picture in mind. It is true that culture can affect an organization's future as well, but strategy is the more direct tool. Furthermore, developing leaders is done in order for them to lead a business, not only to improve human relations.

Is our organization sustainable in the long-term? In which direction should our organization go? What sort of people should lead our organizations? What competencies will they need? How will we help them obtain these competencies? These are the questions that HR professionals should think over and discuss seriously with executives who are truly interested in creating a successful long-term organization. I know that answering these questions is not easy due to many everyday obstacles. However, HR professionals should not forget their very important roles as the people who hold the compass that leads the organization. Hence, traditional leadership development methodology is not the most important part of your roleor, at least, it shouldn't be. Don't forget that you develop leaders, not just classes.

_____

_____

_____

_____

_____

질문 7 여러분 조직(부서)에 필요한 리더를 양성하는 방식에는 어떤 변화가 필요하다고 생각하십니까?

질문 8 앞으로 3년 후 조직(부서)의 방향을 생각해볼 때, 리더들이 공통적으로 갖추어야할 리더 역량은 무엇입니까?

질문 9 조직의 전략을 추구하는 리더십과 기업의 문화를 만드는 리더십은 어떻게 다르다고 생각하십니까?

본 아티클에 대해 여러분은 개인적으로 찬성하십니까? 아니면 반대하십니까? 그 근거는 무엇입니까?

Pros(찬)	Cons(반)
✔	✔
✔	✔
✔	✔
✔	✔
✔	✔

- 본 주제에 대한 여러분의 최종 의견은 무엇입니까?

4. 팀 문화와 수평적 리더십 Team Culture And Horizontal Leadership

Leadership Insights : 팀이나 부서 단위의 문화가 건강할수록 조직 전체의 문화도 건강할 확률이 높습니다. 명확한 목표 설정, 상하/수평 간 활발한 토론이나 정보 공유는 리더십이 만들어내는 팀/부서 문화의 첫걸음입니다.

Is your team culture successful? Why are some teams' performances superior even when they have the same amount of people, space, resources, and recruitment standards as the other teams? This is the first question I usually ask the team leaders of corporations, as almost all corporations are interested in creating high-performing teams.

However, as corporations become more globalized and diverse, creating a successful team culture has been a challenge. In order to build a great team, you need two major ingredients: collaboration, and an effective team leader. It is the latter that we will focus on today. Let's take a look at how team leaders' dysfunctional leadership style can be a hindrance to creating a solid and collaborative team culture and what needs to be done to prevent this.

1) Team culture truly begins when the team is arranged for a single goal.

If there is no clear and challenging team goal, the team will never reach its potential. This goal must be clearly communicated to the employees, so that they know what they are working toward. Furthermore, their feedback on how best to reach this goal should be elicited, in order to increase morale and a sense of ownership. If the leader develops the goal without any input from the rest of the team, the team members will spend their energy pleasing the leader rather than thinking about how best to achieve the goal. This will result in a team culture that is authoritative and not collaborative, which is not desirable because it stifles team members' creativity and initiative.

2) A healthy team culture is one in which team members can voluntarily cooperate and actively negotiate.

When team members feel as though everyone is participating, they will have a psychological connection to their teammates, which, in turn, improves the function of the team. Therefore, it is very important for the leaders to initiate active discussions and meditate conflicts between members with different opinions. Not only do these strategies strengthen members' feelings of ownership and commitment, but they also result in more effective decisions. Eventually, team members should be able to negotiate varying opinions by themselves. This is a great example of how leadership style can affect a team, because some leaders will not allow free discussion or the lively participation and involvement of their members. This results in the leader's monopoly on decision-making and a toxic team culture.

_____

_____

_____

_____

3) A healthy team culture depends on sharing knowledge.

Richard Hackman, a well-known scholar on teams at Harvard University, argues that their ability to create an environment that allows them to support each other is crucial for the team's survival and success. One essential ingredient of a supportive environment is the free flow of information: between team members, and between the leader and the team. In order to ensure that members share information amongst themselves, the leader must create a comfortable and supportive climate. Furthermore, leaders must do their part by sharing information freely with the rest of the team. If leaders keep information to themselves and are not interested in creating a learning environment by distributing information, they will be able to retain all of their power, but their team's culture will turn into a stagnant pond where nobody will be free to breathe and absorb new knowledge.

4) A team's culture is shaped by its leader.

Just as teams become more valuable and effective as they are developed, teams become less valuable and less effective if their development stagnates. Therefore, in order to ensure continued growth, team members have to accept foreign ideas and methods in their field as well as freely contributing their own. The success of an organization depends on the success of its teams, and the success of these teams depends on their ability to innovate. Therefore, autonomy should be given to members so that teams are free to experiment and challenge conventions. Thus, we can easily recognize how important the leaders' roles are, because they are the ones who create the team's culture. If leaders are indifferent to how the culture can be improved, they are not committed to their most important role. Leaders should therefore be mindful of whether they are overly-rigid, as this may be preventing an innovative team culture.

Team spirit and morale is a direct reflection of the team leader's leadership style. If the team leader ensures that members participate in the goal-setting process, cooperate and negotiate amongst themselves, share knowledge with each other, and innovate together, then the team will be a success. Team leaders will shine when they are able to create and maintain an effective team culture by reflecting on their leadership styles and making more of an effort to share power and authority.

질문 10 여러분 팀이나 부서에는 팀원(부서원)들이 집중할 수 있는 뚜렷한 그룹 목표가 있습니까?

질문 11 여러분은 얼마나 오픈된 마인드를 갖고 있습니까? 또 팀이나 부서 내에 토론과 정보 공유를 보다 활성화할 수 있는 방안은 무엇입니까?

질문 12 현재 팀이나 부서의 문화를 돌아볼 때 여러분의 리더십은 어떤 변화가 필요하다고 생각하십니까?

본 아티클에 대해 여러분은 개인적으로 찬성하십니까? 아니면 반대하십니까? 그 근거는 무엇입니까?

Pros(찬)	Cons(반)
✔	✔
✔	✔
✔	✔
✔	✔
✔	✔

• 본 주제에 대한 여러분의 최종 의견은 무엇입니까?

5. 리더의 자기 성찰 Self-Reflective Culture

Leadership Insights : 글로벌 기업과 글로벌 리더가 된다는 것은 기술과 상품, 서비스의 진보를 의미할 뿐만 아니라, 리더들과 기업이 어떠한 글로벌 이미지와 역량을 갖고 있는지, 또 앞으로 가져야 할 것인지를 특정하는 것도 중요합니다.

For the past two weeks, I was in Europe for two workshops, which were held in Finland and the Netherlands, on national and organizational culture. I was able to meet about 30 professors, consultants and corporate instructors from all over the world.

During these two workshops, I had many opportunities to hear foreigners discussing Korean national culture and corporate culture as they saw it. Even now that the workshops have finished, these discussions linger in my mind: opinions from pundits from other countries led me to reflect on who we Koreans really are and whether we see ourselves objectively and fairly.

In Finland, the foreign participants talked about the educational systems in their own countries, and asked the Finnish people what the distinguishing characteristics of their educational system were. A professor from Finland answered without hesitation, "We tend to think that effective education teaches how to study instead of emphasizing the amount of study or the content itself. Thus, schools do not give a lot of homework at most, two or three hours after school. We de-emphasize memorization: after all, knowledge is accessible so easily today."

This simple answer made me question whether our educational system is really as good as we think, considering that Korean students spend much more time studying to get similar results (as determined by global rankings each year).

Doing well does not require doing a lot. Do we not understand this, or do we understand yet refuse to change? Or is it rather that we know we need to change but we don't know how? These questions even lead to a broader question about Korean society as a whole: Are we truly doing well?

In the Netherlands, I had the opportunity to see a Swedish professor and a Dutch professor talking about Korean culture. Both of them were knowledgeable about intercultural management and have been teaching the subject for more than 20-30 years. They, as did many others, talked about the rapid growth in Korea's economy over the past several decades. However, some of their knowledge about Korean culture came from non-Korean sources. For example, one professor showed me how Korean culture is interpreted in the world and how Korean culture developed into its present incarnation.

What surprised me was that the material he showed me was based on what a Japanese professor had said about Korean society, the development of the Korean economy and its corporations, and the strengths and weaknesses of Korea. In fact, many people I met during the workshop understood Korea from the perspective of Japanese professors.

This second experience pushed me to another question: Do we see ourselves as others see us? Are we making an effort to close the gap between how we see ourselves and how others see us that is, to see ourselves more objectively? And who defines us do we, or do others? Are we making an effort to present ourselves to the world in a comprehensible way, instead of letting the Japanese, or others, do it?

Recently, I delivered a workshop to several dozen global managers from twenty different countries in one of the largest companies in Korea. Many of the participants highlighted how tech-savvy they found Korean corporations to be. However, on the negative side, they also pointed out that Korean managers and directors still have excessively top-down mindsets and management styles.

Whenever I deliver global workshops to foreign participants, these are invariably their reactions. Given that global organizations cannot become successful by merely having great technology, we need to reconsider what we should pay more attention to. Products, services, and IT are the ultimate deliverables and their importance cannot be underestimated; however, it is people that increase or decrease the value of these deliverables. If human beings are valued, they will reflect this in the quality of their work and the products and services that they produce.

Furthermore, without taking into account the wants and needs of different kinds of people all over the world, Korean corporations cannot become true global companies. Thus, Korean corporations need to invest as much in the global development of their managers as they do in tangible deliverables.

How we look at ourselves matters not only because it determines how we will grow in the future, but also because it determines whether we will grow desirably and successfully, which finally means globally.

At the same time, how we will help other people in the world see us is as important as how we see ourselves. Finally, when how we see ourselves is the same as how others see us, we can find better ways to grow. We focused on how to develop ourselves over the past several decades; we now need to figure out how to develop ourselves well for the upcoming future. Successful change always begins with a clear direction and a long-term vision. Repeated mistakes are not mistakes, but a sign of a lack of capability. Change without self-reflection does not lead to a sustainable future.

질문 13 세계적으로 대한민국이 글로벌 리더십을 발휘하기 위해서는 국가 차원에서 어떤 변화가 필요하다고 생각하십니까?

질문 14 회사를 대표하여 글로벌 시장에 진출한다면, 다른 나라 사람들에게 여러분 회사의 어떤 면을 소개하시겠습니까?

질문 15 앞으로 여러분의 회사가 보다 글로벌한 기업이 되려면 조직 내 리더들은 어떤 변화가 필요합니까?

본 아티클에 대해 여러분은 개인적으로 찬성하십니까? 아니면 반대하십니까? 그 근거는 무엇입니까?

Pros(찬)	Cons(반)
✔	✔
✔	✔
✔	✔
✔	✔
✔	✔

- 본 주제에 대한 여러분의 최종 의견은 무엇입니까?

6. 질문을 사랑하는 리더십 Cultivating 'Questioning Culture'

Leadership Insights : 한국의 기업들은 많은 장점에도 불구하고 리더들이 아랫사람들에게 질문을 많이 허용하지 않는 문화를 갖고 있습니다. 결론적으로 토론과 의견 공유가 적은 편이며, 이는 다양한 인종과 사람들이 모이는 글로벌 기업 문화에서는 개선이 시급한 부분입니다.

If you are always being questioned but are never allowed to ask questions of your own, you may develop a tendency to be defensive or to avoid commitments. On the other hand, if you are free to ask questions, you may become more active, autonomous and self-motivated. The act of questioning has the ability to create independent thinkers. Since many Korean companies are attempting to fix their corporate cultures, I would like to explore how a "questioning culture" can help corporations and people become more participative and develop leadership qualities.

According to Clayton Christensen, a professor at Harvard Business School, business leaders think questioning is "inefficient" because they are anxious to "get things done. "This insight matches how leaders and managers behave in Korean corporations: since they are responsible for the completion of their work, they are usually quick to decide and act. It is indeed true that ordering subordinates to follow their directives takes much less time than asking for their opinions or ideas. This is why it is difficult for a questioning culture to take hold in our corporations.

However, an investment in a questioning culture will be well worth it. The business environment is changing, companies' strategies are changing, and so the competencies needed for employees are changing. Thus, Korean corporations need to pursue organizational cultures that will allow them to fully function in this ever-transforming business world. Given all this, helping employees become more creative and self-determined is exactly what companies should do.

A.G Lafley, the executive chairman of P&G who revitalized the company under the slogan of "The consumer is boss," was famous for allotting two-thirds of all of his meetings to listening to his subordinates' opinions. He asserted that as you climb the corporate ladder, you should listen to your subordinates more. He is regarded as one of the most lauded CEOs in history, and his management philosophy was not hierarchical, but rather horizontal. When CEOs or leaders are open to the ideas and opinions of their subordinates like Lafley was, organizations will become a place where self-leadership flourishes and ownership is shared by employees and leaders alike. One part of truly listening to employees is allowing them to ask questions.

Questioning is as powerful as listening in creating a culture in which employees will develop autonomy and become more participative, committed, and engaged. When they are valued and respected, they feel free to express more creative ideas and come up with strategies to grow their companies.

How, then, to create this questioning culture? Reflecting on these three points is a good start: First, leaders and managers should make it acceptable for their juniors to answer that they "don't know" if they truly don't know the answer to a question.

Second, leaders and mangers should ask positive questions instead of using questions to discourage and dis-empower their subordinates. Third, leaders and managers should know that the answer itself is less important than the process of pursuing an answer. If they are forced to say the "right answers," employees will be like tamed lambs who conform to their leaders instead of thinking independently.

Nationally and in organizations, Korean people live under a hierarchical culture, which may make asking questions to one's superiors or one's inferiors seem unnecessary or out of place. However, our quickly-changing world demands flexibility and punishes adherence to the status quo that is built on already-existing answers. We should be more open to and more courageous in accepting wholly new possibilities and unprecedented solutions. Therefore, let's create a questioning culture where all people can explore new ideas and develop self-leadership.

질문 16 여러분은 (자주) 질문하는 직원에게 어떤 태도를 보이십니까?

질문 17 직접 주관하는 회의에서 여러분이 경청하는 분량은 어느 정도입니까?

질문 18 여러분은 동료나 부하직원의 반대의견(Pushback)을 얼마나 허용하는 편입니까?

본 아티클에 대해 여러분은 개인적으로 찬성하십니까? 아니면 반대하십니까? 그 근거는 무엇입니까?

Pros(찬)	Cons(반)
✔	✔
✔	✔
✔	✔
✔	✔
✔	✔

• 본 주제에 대한 여러분의 최종 의견은 무엇입니까?

7. 수직적 리더들 'Ggondae Leadership'

Leadership Insights : 글로벌 기업을 지향한다면 수직보다는 수평적 문화가 보다 적합합니다. 그런 면에서 수직적 문화에서 어울리는 행동과, 수평적 문화에서 어울리는 리더 행동을 구분하는 것은 의미가 깊습니다.

Are you a leader? Then I would like to ask you this question: How aware are you of what your employees think? Specifically, how aware are you of what your employees think about you? An essential element of being a good leader is understanding your own image.

Some world-famous corporate leaders are notorious for their poor communication and authoritarian leadership style. According to Alex Bracetti's "Horrible Bosses: The Worst Tech CEOs of All Time," Steve Ballmer, Meg Whitman and Carly Fiorina are infamous for these negative qualities as well as their arrogant disregard and impolite treatment of employees. Of course, one might argue that leaders' being authoritarian and unpleasant doesn't matter as long as they are creating profits. However, this style of leadership is, in the long-term, not desirable, as it makes leaders unable to count on unity and loyalty from their employees. Indeed, leaders like that may be the objects of complaints and even cause employees to leave the organization.

Thus, leaders must be aware of what communication styles they are using and what their reputation is as well as how to improve both. Changes in the leader affect changes in the organizational climate, and so if a leader wishes to change the organizational climate, he or she would do well to start from within.

For instance, leaders must acknowledge how they speak to their employees. If leaders are aware of what facial expressions they are using when speaking to their subordinates, subordinates may be more genuinely inclined to listen and cooperate. If leaders consciously try to control their emotions when upset, they will be more skillful in dealing with their employees and thus create an atmosphere in which more supportive dialogues will occur. If leaders make sure to use professional tones of voice, followers will begin feeling valued and listened to. These small changes are powerful because they make employees feel secure and encourage their active participation.

What else can leaders do to change their images? Specifically, since Korean (and other Asian) corporate cultures are known for being excessively " top-down," how can leaders from these countries undo long-standing reputations? Here are some tips to consider.

1) If you consider the ages or positions of employees first and then use non-honorific expressions based on that, fix it.

2) If you point out employees' weaknesses and failures rather than their strengths and accomplishments, fix it.

3) If you ask employees to express their opinions but then stick only to your own ideas, fix it.

4) If you really hate the people who do not appear for a get-together after the work due

to their personal issues, fix it.

5) If you hold grudges against subordinates who opposed your ideas, fix it.

6) If you micromanage, fix it.

7) If you do not control your emotions around your employees, fix it.

Anyone who does not do these things is in danger of being seen as a "Ggondae" that is, a middle-aged man who tries to use authority and power to lead people instead of humane influence. This derogatory term is generally used by younger generations to deride their older authoritarian mangers and leaders in Korea.

Horizontal leadership and culture do not come without effort. They require that leaders be approved, loved and respected by their employees. As more and more leaders become recognized positively by their employees, more companies will become great places to work for. This is why leaders must actively change their leadership styles to positively affect their company's corporate culture.

질문 19 여러분은 자신의 리더십 스타일에 대해 어떻게 평가하십니까?

질문 20 여러분은 리더로서 자신의 커뮤니케이션 스타일에 대해 어떻게 평가하십니까?

질문 21 조직이 보다 수평적인 조직문화를 갖추기 위해 조직 내 리더의 행동에는 어떤 변화가 필요합니까?

본 아티클에 대해 여러분은 개인적으로 찬성하십니까? 아니면 반대하십니까? 그 근거는 무엇입니까?

Pros(찬)	Cons(반)
✔	✔
✔	✔
✔	✔
✔	✔
✔	✔

- 본 주제에 대한 여러분의 최종 의견은 무엇입니까?

---

8. 정답이 없다고 말할 수 있는 리더십 Organizations Without Answers

> Leadership Insights : 시장 환경과 경쟁의 패턴이 변화함에도 불구하고 조직들이 기존의 접근법과 솔루션을 고집하는 것은 기업 성장의 발목을 잡는 주요 요인이 됩니다. 그런 면에서 지속적인 자기 성찰이 필요합니다.

Which organization has a better chance of survival: organizations that already have answers, or organizations that are looking for them?

If we see organizations as having fixed problems to solve, then of course organizations with answers have the advantage; however, if we see organizations as growing organisms, this advantage turns into an impediment, as an organization's current answers are not going to be appropriate in every situation.

Given this, organizations must be willing to let go of solutions that have previously worked when the situation has changed. This kind of flexibility will be crucial in creating the kind of culture necessary to propel the organization to success.

I see this often in my work as an organizational consultant and instructor when for-profit and non-profit organizations call me in to discuss and resolve their problems. What I find most striking is not what sort of problems they want to tackle, but what sort of processes they would like to use in order to solve them. Based on their corporate governance, management style, culture, and history, they tend to favor very different approaches. Furthermore, most of them have a "one-size-fits-all" approach that they are already accustomed to and that they prefer to use in any situation regardless of the context. It may be reassuring to them to stick to a familiar path, but being unable to adjust one's methods and adapt to the circumstances severely limits one's chances of success.

A few years ago, I visited an organization that had called me in to address an internal organizational conflict that they told me was a delicate situation. Since these problems were inter-departmental, we naturally assumed that we needed to hear from the team leaders and members of both sides. However, the people in charge the training staff told me that we would not, in fact, be doing any kind of interview process; rather, we would simply deliver training to both teams. The training staff would then claim to monitor the behavior of both teams to analyze whether or not they had sufficiently changed after the training, but this would actually just be a pretext for firing one of the team leaders, as this leader was already disliked by the president of the company.

It was not totally clear, the training staff admitted, which team was the real cause of the problem, but given this tension between the leader and the president, it would be faster and easier to just get rid of the "problem" leader, which would then solve the inter-departmental conflict. The fact that the training staff naturally assumed that this is what the CEO would want was indicative of their larger culture and how they normally solved issues. Instead of taking a hard look at their internal problems, they wanted a quick resolution through using the methods that they traditionally used.

This is not, by any means, an extreme case of how corporations handle their obstacles. Many organizations do not want to look into real issues because they already have their own solutions or answers that they would like to use regardless of the result of the situational diagnosis. Of course, they already know what kind of side effects their approaches may have. However, inertia tempts organizations to stick to the beaten path without thinking about its efficacy. Furthermore, problem-solvers often feel that it's safer to follow the precedents set by their corporate history or the tastes of their leadership team and CEO.

There are some common themes among corporations that fall into this trap. First, there tends to be an emphasis on communication between the training staff and upper-level leaders, with little or no input from employees. Second, these organizations tend to value short-term performance at the expense of other organizational perspectives. Third, they have a culture in which it is a habit to be conscious of how or in what way leaders want people to pursue solutions. These three traits bring significant disadvantages.

For one, there will be lower morale and engagement in employees, who will feel disempowered due to being always told how to approach problems. Furthermore, there will be misalignment between the chief executives and the employees, because the directions of the training staff will be based solely on their assumptions of what the executives want, with no reasoning or logic made explicit to the employees, who will then not know why they're doing what they're doing. Finally, the behaviors of the organization will become fixed and inflexible, making it more difficult to innovate. Thus, the organizational synergy that can be created when the top and bottom layers merge never appears.

This is not all. If organizations have ready-made solutions or answers, employees will become passive, and this passivity may even make its way into the organizational identity. According to Albert & Whetten, organizational identity is "a collective understanding of what the clear values and characteristics of the organization are." When employees are always told to be passive, they will begin to consciously or unconsciously believe that this is the kind of behavior that the organization values, resulting in their thinking, feeling, and behaving in a fixed and predictable way. In addition, when these organizational identities are hardened and woven into the fabric of organizational daily lives, it becomes difficult for organizations to change or adapt because all of their energies are put toward currying favor with their leadership. This will eventually result in feelings of division between leaders and employees because leaders do not truly listen to their employees.

Tannenbaum and Schmidt were some of the first theorists to make use of this idea of changing one's leadership patterns based on the situation. Their Leadership Continuum Theorem claimed that applying leadership styles flexibly based on the circumstances and the level of organizational development is necessary in order to move an organization forward. It is crucial that leaders are authentically interested in accurately diagnosing the situation, adapting themselves to it, and communicating with their employees. Leaders can go even further than this and give authority and freedom to their employees, which will result in an employee body that is itself more flexible, adaptive, innovative, and creative.

As illustrated above, organizations with pre-made answers tend to become fixed and stuck, which is not conducive to a healthy organizational culture. Those who prepare the very answers that their leaders prefer are accomplices in their organization's stagnation and collapse. Thus, it is important to create an organization that does not come with ready-made answers and is open to finding a different answer for every unique situation. It is especially important to make sure that this openness becomes a habit; otherwise, ready-made answers become part of the company's culture, which means that it will be very difficult to change. According to Rob Goffee, a professor at London Business School, a company's culture is often ingrained so deeply that employees can't really see it clearly until it becomes so toxic that they realize it must change but, by that point, it's too late. To prevent this from happening, innovation must be consciously practiced.

질문 22 여러분의 조직이 쉽게 바꾸지 못하는 관행 한 가지는 무엇입니까?

질문 23 여러분이 당면한 조직 내 문제를 하나 떠올려 보십시오. 기존과 다른 방식으로 이 문제에 접근한다면 어떤 새로운 접근이 가능합니까?

질문 24 여러분 회사의 사람들이 보다 Open-Mind를 갖기 위해서는 어떤 개선 방법이 효과적입니까?

본 아티클에 대해 여러분은 개인적으로 찬성하십니까? 아니면 반대하십니까? 그 근거는 무엇입니까?

Pros(찬)	Cons(반)
✔	✔
✔	✔
✔	✔
✔	✔
✔	✔

- 본 주제에 대한 여러분의 최종 의견은 무엇입니까?

9. 파도에게 배우는 조직의 교훈 Organizational Lessons From Ocean's Waves

Leadership Insights : 특정 문제에 집중하기 보다 조직의 현황을 업종이라는 큰 그림 차원에서 보고 필요한 변화 유무를 파악하며, 이에 연결되는 리더십의 변화를 정의 내릴 때, 보다 다양하고 현실적인 가치들을 반영할 수 있습니다.

A few weeks ago, I stayed at a hotel near Haeundae beach to rest, having started to feel fatigue from my work with client organizations. Looking through the hotel window, I was able to observe the movement of the changing sea waves and relate them to organizations. I then found that my fatigue came from my own perspective and not from the organizations themselves.

1) Organizations shine with diverse colors and chroma, just like sea waves.

Organizations are composed of diverse members, diverse competencies and diverse roles. Thus, when we try to measure organizations with a single perspective, we cannot see them in all their complexity. Given this, you need the broadest possible definition of an organization in order to accurately define it. This is because your definition of the largest traits or characteristics of an organization will affect the effectiveness of the movement and direction of an organization. Furthermore, looking at an organization too closely, without looking at the bigger picture, can lead to errors. To come back to the waves metaphor, some people may highlight and magnify red, others may do the same for green, while in reality, organizations have diverse colors. All in all, the ability to figure out what is really needed and then place it in a larger context will lead to success. Paradoxically, the more diverse an organization is, the broader and simpler definition it will need in order to capture all of that diversity.

2) Organizations are dynamic and not static, just like sea waves.

We commonly use metaphors for defining organizations: organizations are like machines, we say, or organizations are like a family. However, just as sea waves differ based on the time of day, the wind and the sunshine, organizations take on new forms, sometimes subtly or sometimes dramatically. Sometimes they maintain a peaceful stability; other times, the wind whips them up into raging waves. No organization is completely static, and all organizations change constantly. An organization may seem static in the moment, but if you zoom out and observe over a long period of time, you will see that organizations are, in fact, in a perpetual state of flux. Being able to recognize this accurately and take this into consideration when deciding whether to sail left or right is crucial for organizational success.

3) Leadership is also always changing, just like sea waves.

We commonly say that our leaders are a certain "type" or "style" and that they cannot change easily. However, the leadership of an organization is actually always changing, whether for better or worse. And based on these changes, the direction of organizations change, either a lot or just a little, and so do organizational strategy and culture. Thus, being able to accurately see these changes even the smallest ones will allow one to truly contribute to an organization. As the case stands, leaders need to check whether they are leaning too much to one side or another, and whether they are focused on the characteristics that the organization and its industry require. This is why looking at the change of a whole ocean is much more important than looking at the change of the small waves.

In conclusion, what we should not forget is that there are various types of sounds in organizations, just like in the sea. The sound of pleasure, the sound of fatigue, the sound of accomplishment, the sound of fighting, the sound of groaning, the sound of injustice, et cetera. When they are seen as they are and reacted to appropriately, organizations can become more successful. If these sounds are ignored, organizational culture will eventually be destroyed just as human beings, ignoring the sound of the rising ocean, will eventually drown. An organization in any industry should not make the sound of stillness at night but rather the vigorous sound of seagulls during the day. Thus, organizations need to learn from the waves of the ocean, since they are filled with invaluable lessons.

_____

_____

_____

_____

_____

질문 25 업종의 변화를 고려할 때 여러분 조직의 변화 현황은 어떻습니까?

질문 26 여러분 조직이 겪고 있는 변화는 점진적입니까? 아니면 급진적입니까? 각각의 장단점은 무엇입니까?

질문 27 조직 내 보다 다양한 목소리를 반영하기 위해서 리더들이 할 수 있는 것은 무엇입니까?

본 아티클에 대해 여러분은 개인적으로 찬성하십니까? 아니면 반대하십니까? 그 근거는 무엇입니까?

Pros(찬)	Cons(반)
✓	✓
✓	✓
✓	✓
✓	✓
✓	✓

• 본 주제에 대한 여러분의 최종 의견은 무엇입니까?

> Leadership Insights : 글로벌 기업 문화일수록 실수가 허용되고, 실수로부터 배우며, 리더 또한 실무자로부터 배우는 학습 문화를 스스로 조성하려고 노력합니다.

While visiting a variety of client organizations as an organizational development consultant, I was able to discover one truth about corporate culture. Organizations generally think of their employees as objects whose deficiencies are theirs to correct and improve upon. Thus, corporations usually attempt to eliminate or remold their shortcomings. The focus is on teaching managers how their employees should be changed.

However, there are two problems with this perspective.

First, if corporations emphasize what their employees lack, this is deeply discouraging to their employees, who will then think of themselves as "problem children" and lose confidence rapidly. This loss of confidence is devastating for the company, because confidence supports employees in finding new possibilities and solutions to challenges during turbulent times. Furthermore, a lack of confidence destroys spirit, enthusiasm and willingness to sacrifice.

Second, this affects more than just individual employees: it also influences the organizational climate. A dark and heavy atmosphere will smother the workplace like a thick blanket, and will eventually grow into a dysfunctional mass that the organization will try to get rid of every day. Employees will begin to regard their organization as tiring and annoying, a place of denial, refusal, problems and issues, perhaps even as an enemy. Consequently, this organization will become a place where negativity meets negativity and weakens potential and possibilities.tiring and annoying, a place of denial, refusal, problems and issues, perhaps even as an enemy. Consequently, this organization will become a place where negativity meets negativity and weakens potential and possibilities. On the other hand, there are some corporations which focus on human beings and deliberately build their confidence instead of highlighting their weaknesses. They usually know how to utilize the varying aptitudes of their employees. They believe people contain infinite possibilities and have the potential to transform. They do not think their employees should be forcefully trained or educated, but rather help in identifying their own strengths and weaknesses. They place a great deal of importance on hearing their employees' voices.

When organizations behave like this, they will be filled with positive energy, which will translate into a "can-do" spirit and strong self-esteem in their employees. This is what truly helps an organization grow and improve. After all, what empowers organizations is the attitudes that their employees have about their organization, the attitudes that their managers and leaders have about their employees, and an atmosphere of self-analysis and experimentation that allows for participation and innovation.

It is not easy to create excellent employees and organizations when employees feel disrespected. Positive culture and leadership are as important as business strategies, marketing and brands.

This means that a "teaching culture" that is, a culture aimed at "fixing" employees does not suffice in creating a successful organization, since it will create a demotivational environment. Rather, organizations should try to create a "learning culture," that emphasizes what employees and managers should learn from each other both horizontally and vertically. Showing mutual respect, understanding and consideration will energize the employees and enrich the organization.

How, then, to cultivate a learning culture instead of a teaching culture? According to Dr. Carol Dweck, a professor at Stanford University who is renowned for her research in motivation, building a growth mindset is essential in helping employees learn from mistakes and actively seek out challenges. In addition, letting employees expand their perspectives by learning from their mistakes is crucial to creating a true learning culture. For example, when we think of Google, we tend to think of it as a genius organization that is successful because of intrinsic abilities. However, this is not true. Rather, they have a tendency to utilize their failures as stepping-stones to construct better opportunities. Google Buzz tanked; however, this experience was wisely made use of to create a better outcome, Google Plus, which was more successful. Furthermore, when an organization and its employees become familiar with the concept of a learning culture, they should not remain there. Leaders should get involved and acknowledge that there are things that they can learn from their employees, too. If leaders lead by example, with humility, a learning culture will automatically set in. Let's not try to teach. Let's learn from each other.

질문 28 여러분은 지금까지 리더로서 직원들을 문제 자체로 보는 경향이 컸나요? 아니면 문제의 해결자로 대해 오셨나요?

66

질문 29 긍정적인 조직문화와 리더십은 어느 정도의 중요성이 있다고 생각하십니까?

질문 30 혁신에 실패하는 기업일수록 실수를 엄하게 다스리는 경향이 있습니다. 여러분 조직의 리더들은 직원들이 실패로부터 배우는 문화에 대해서 얼마나 관대하십니까?

본 아티클에 대해 여러분은 개인적으로 찬성하십니까? 아니면 반대하십니까? 그 근거는 무엇입니까?

Pros(찬)	Cons(반)
✔	✔
✔	✔
✔	✔
✔	✔
✔	✔

• 본 주제에 대한 여러분의 최종 의견은 무엇입니까?

11. 현장에서 배우는 리더들 New Corporate Learning Culture

> Leadership Insights : 리더들이 직원들의 단순 교육 참여보다 현장에서 실행을 지원하려고 돕고, 교재보다 현장 문제를 대입시켜 이해하도록 하며, 리더 자신의 관점 뿐만 아니라 조직에 대한 직원들 다수의 관점에 관심을 가질수록 조직은 보다 건강해집니다.

Organizations are interested in helping their employees upgrade their work or leadership capabilities. That is why they provide a variety of training.

However, since it is difficult to accurately measure the effectiveness of the training, the satisfaction level of the participants tends to be measured instead. Because of this, many organizations believe that workshops that end with a lot of laughter and positive comments are successful and effective.

Looking more closely at whether participants are actually increasing their knowledge, sharpening their skills, or changing their attitudes, though, much of this training does not deserve compliments. Sometimes, it has no effect at all due to the participants' lack of motivation to change themselves because they were too busy laughing and doing a lot of fun activities. What, then, would effective training look like?

Corporate training provides training materials and auxiliary aides to help participants fully understand the topics. Participants themselves add to this wealth of information with their own notes. However, this gives the impression that the point of the training is to acquire and absorb new knowledge. Participants tend to forget what is truly significant: how to apply what they learn for themselves.

Given this, we can easily recognize that participants will learn more when they think about what they need to do and how they need to change instead of just blindly accepting the content. Thus, providing training materials which are filled with information and data will be useless and will actually hinder the participants from thinking about how to use the essential points of the acquired knowledge in their workplace.

In fact, I once conducted a full-day workshop without any materials at all. I didn't prepare textbooks, handouts, or even a short summary of what we were supposed to learn; instead, I simply prepared 10 topics for discussion.

The participants and I talked about current issues and problems in their organization and the opinions that I had collected from them during a diagnosis before the workshop. This led to a discussion about the main causes of the issues and what some potential solutions might be.

Since there were no right or wrong answers, the participants were free to voice their own opinions and sometimes argue in order to scrutinize the effectiveness of various approaches. I prepared only several meaningful pictures that I was able to show to help remind the participants of the importance of the topic under discussion. After each round of discussion, we concluded with agreements, the implementation of which the majority of participants supported.

Traditionally, leaders have thought that their employees should be more knowledgeable and more self-correcting. Leaders even tend to think their employees are the primary cause of their organizational problems.

However, exploring organizational issues at a deeper level has usually led me to the conclusion that leaders' pejorative attitudes toward their employees are causing much larger problems. That is why leaders need to learn not about a new method of strategic planning, a new culture, or new management theories, but about what they are doing and how they need to change.

They should learn not only from their own training sessions but from sessions for their employees even when they are not present. That is, training should include frank discussions of leaders without their presence. If leaders are absent when they are being discussed, then employees will feel comfortable giving honest feedback. This requires a lot of courage for leaders, because there may be many truths that are painful to hear.

However, if employees give accurate descriptions of what is happening in the organization and why, this perspective could be invaluable. It is true that when employees are free to talk about their leaders' misjudgment, misconduct, and mismanagement, leaders may not like what their employees are saying. However, this kind of feedback is the most effective information much more effective than that given by outside coaches and instructors.

After all, employees have been diagnosing their leaders for a much longer time and with a much larger poll size. When what employees want is aligned with what leaders and organizations want, organizations will have greater success. That is why leaders need to learn from sessions even when they are absent.

I have visited more than several hundred companies over many years. Based on my workshops, consulting services, and casual talks with corporate personnel, almost all organizations have problems that come from not knowing the reality of their situations, what direction they really need to go in, and whether they are truly cohesive. This is not so surprising: usually, truth does not appear without being deliberately sought, since truth is covered under the dust of routine, of work, and of relationships.

To find true success, companies need look to themselves as opposed to always looking at and trying to copy others. Truths about your organization exist somewhere, even if you cannot see them right now, and effective training can help to uncover them.

_____

_____

_____

_____

_____

질문 31 교육을 받은 후 여러분은 직원들이 어느 정도 교육 내용을 현실에 반영할 수 있도록 돕고 있습니까?

질문 32 일방적인 교육을 제공하는 대신에 조직의 현황을 토론하는 자리를 갖는다고 생각해 보십시오. Top 3 토론 주제는 무엇입니까?

질문 33 여러분 조직에서 리더들이 생각하는 것과 직원들이 생각하는 것 중 가장 큰 차이를 보이는 부분은 무엇입니까?

본 아티클에 대해 여러분은 개인적으로 찬성하십니까? 아니면 반대하십니까? 그 근거는 무엇입니까?

Pros(찬)	Cons(반)
✔	✔
✔	✔
✔	✔
✔	✔
✔	✔

• 본 주제에 대한 여러분의 최종 의견은 무엇입니까?

---

12. 회의 문화를 이끄는 리더십 Meetings – A Skill Or A Culture?

Leadership Insights : 리더들이 회의를 진행하는 효과적인 스킬에서 나아가 자신의 리더십과 자신의 행동이 만드는 조직문화적 측면에 중점하게 되면 회의 문화 혁신이 보다 성공적일 수 있습니다.

Recently, I had an interview with a newspaper regarding my book on meetings. The reporter was interested mainly in getting the gist of how to conduct a good or "effective" meeting. What struck me was that her questions e.g., how to run a meeting smoothly, how to conduct a discussion, how to lead decision-making, how to follow up all implied that a meeting is a discrete tool, something to be used in service of a greater aim. However, this is a common misconception: a meeting is not just a skill, but rather a microcosm of your organization's culture itself.

Thus, a well-led meeting is not merely an example of a leader's skill in conducting meetings. Rather, meetings are leadership itself, and organizational culture itself. If we view meetings as "cultures," our approach towards them begins to differ significantly.

If meetings are a matter of skill, then the following statements should be true:
- It is possible to improve the planning, conducting, and following-up of meetings as independent skills.

- If leaders, subordinates and new employees are educated, there should be substantial advancements for all, regardless of their ranks and positions.
- Those world-famous companies that are generally viewed as having desirable meeting

cultures, such 3M, Honda, Disney, and Google, achieved these cultures through skills training.

- Companies that have gone through meeting skills trainings should show that their meetings have improved correspondingly.

On the other hand, if meetings are a matter of culture, then the following statements should be true:

- One must change the behaviors, opinions, and even values of people in order to change meetings.

- It is essential to focus on educating topline executives, including CEOs. The mindsets of senior management should take priority over those of new employees and subordinates. Without this, subordinates and new employees cannot show effective meeting skills because their leaders' authoritative attitudes will not allow them.

- Those world-famous companies that are generally recognized as having a desirable meeting culture achieved it as a natural result of pursuing a strong cultural perspective.

- Companies that have gone through meeting skills trainings have made little to no improvement with their meetings if they just focused on skills trainings.

Thus, all that said above, it is clear that meetings are a representative part of organizational culture.

As an organizational consultant, I do conduct a training on improving meetings in organizations; however, I always try to approach meetings in terms of organizational culture. One frequent objection to this approach is that changing an organization's culture is a substantial and difficult project, and that it is far easier to focus merely on skills. My response is that one must rather see this as an opportunity to sit down and take time to define the characteristics of one's meetings, the symbol of one's corporate culture. People can lead their corporate climate in the direction they want by clarifying the corporate culture and meeting culture that they wish to have in the future.

It goes without saying that when organizations do not have corporate cultures that fit their business strategies, the visions of their leadership, and the demands of their customers and industries, their competitiveness will regress and they will eventually become dysfunctional.

All in all, purposefully defining what a desirable meeting looks like in one's organization is the simplest way to change organizational culture. Since meetings are the primary time when leadership is publicly executed, they define the way people in organizations work and follow. Thus, meetings give birth to the philosophies and values with which companies approach their customers.

It is never too late. Let's design the meeting culture that your organizations need and want. I look forward to seeing this day becoming the first day that CEOs and executives see their meetings as a manifestation of their corporate cultures and their unique organizational DNA.

질문 34 회의의 효과성은 조직문화, 리더십, 리더의 스킬 중 어느 것과 가장 연관이 깊습니까?

질문 35 조직문화의 관점에서 여러분 조직의 회의 모습이 개선되려면 어떤 부분의 변화가 가장 시급합니까?

질문 36 여러분이 리더로서 진행하는 회의 모습을 개선한다면 어떤 변화 방향을 설정하시겠습니까?

본 아티클에 대해 여러분은 개인적으로 찬성하십니까? 아니면 반대하십니까? 그 근거는 무엇입니까?

Pros(찬)	Cons(반)
✔	✔
✔	✔
✔	✔
✔	✔
✔	✔

• 본 주제에 대한 여러분의 최종 의견은 무엇입니까?

13. 리더 – 권위를 내려놓다 Lowering Walls

> Leadership Insights : 보다 글로벌 기업으로 나아가기 위해서는 리더와 직원 간의 높은 장벽, 리더의 마이크로매니지먼트, 권한 위임 스킬 부족을 무엇보다 먼저 개선해야 합니다.

"Drop it and do as I say." Can you guess in what situation these words were spoken? You might assume that this was said to a very small child by a parent or teacher, but, in fact, this was said to an employee by his manager. Even worse, this situation is far from unique: when I visit client companies and discuss what actions or words bother employees the most, they often cite these kinds of unilateral orders from managers to their subordinates. This indicates that there are still many managers who want their juniors to do whatever they tell them to do without talking back or trying to have their own authority.

Foreigners who have experienced Korean corporate culture sometimes describe it as "suffocating" or "embarrassing." Those words might sound extreme, but we can guess how tiring it is to survive in the Korean corporate world. This is, after all, an environment in which something like "how dare he" or "how dare she" is said if a new hire has the audacity to leave the office earlier than the team leader. If you have ever worked for a Korean company, you will immediately recognize the atmosphere that I'm trying to describe. This hierarchical corporate culture makes Korean employees more exhausted and frustrated than their counterparts in many other countries.

Compare these organizational conditions to those of companies in, for example, the United States. According to a recent Gallup survey, more than 80 percent of U.S. organizations are undoing conventional hierarchical structures and about 84 percent of U.S. employees are "matrixed," which means that they do not have to cling to specific roles and tasks. Instead, they move around to support different projects as team members on various teams. This improves employee flexibility and autonomy, even if it engenders a few disadvantages such as unclear roles, lack of accountability, and dedication to some extent.

If, as has been proven by countless studies, hierarchical culture weakens autonomy, authority and volunteerism, we should do what will help employees be energized and engaged, rather than oppressing them with micromanagement. If not, Korean employees will continue to be fatigued, and they will likely have a tendency to avoid innovation, which is always accompanied by risk. As a result, our industries will be less competitive due to their weaker ability to adapt to unpredictable challenges in the future.

One possible solution to the negative impacts of hierarchical culture is helping managers improve their delegation skills. This will lead managers and supervisors to pay more attention to employees' strengths and talents and will create an environment in which managers and supervisors do not wield absolute power. Rather, they will listen more to their employees, and respect their decision-making. Over time, a culture will organically form in which any person who has a good idea feels free to speak up. Take Google as an example: Google developed their own systems such as Google Caf, TGIF, Googlegeist, and employee evaluation of managers to help employees exchange more ideas, get direct answers from managers and top leaders, and choose which managers they wanted to take on as role models. Google's productive organizational culture is a direct result of their willingness to lower the wall between managers and employees.

However, according to the late London Business School Professor John Hunt, 30 percent of managers regard themselves as being good at delegation, but only one-third of that 30 percent are considered good delegators by their subordinates. Therefore, many managers and leaders still do not want to empower their employees by delegating authority and tasks. The more they do, the more we need to try.

We live in a hyper-connected society, in which information spreads freely. However, the Korean corporate world looks like it still is entrapped by the old dogma. Judging from the rest of the world, our industries will flourish more when they make all the stakeholders their employees, managers, executives, regulators and customers truly connected. We live in a world where sharing power and authority trumps hierarchy. Let's be ready to delegate and listen.

🖊

_____

_____

_____

_____

질문 37 여러분이 리더로서 조직 내 또는 부서 내 내려놓아야 할 권위적인 모습이 있다면 그것은 무엇입니까?

질문 38 마이크로매니저(Micromanager)인 리더들이 조직문화, 조직의 성장에 미치는 영향은 무엇입니까?

질문 39 리더들이 권한 위임(Empowerment)과 역할 위임(Delegation)을 효과적으로 이행할 수 있는 방법은 무엇입니까?

본 아티클에 대해 여러분은 개인적으로 찬성하십니까? 아니면 반대하십니까? 그 근거는 무엇입니까?

Pros(찬)	Cons(반)
✔	✔
✔	✔
✔	✔
✔	✔
✔	✔

• 본 주제에 대한 여러분의 최종 의견은 무엇입니까?

14. 팀과 부서 간 장벽을 허무는 리더 Busting Silos To Unify

> Leadership Insights : 조직이 전체로서 경쟁력을 발휘하고 전략을 구사하는 데는 팀/부서/계열사 간 협력과 소통은 필수이며, 리더들은 구체적인 소통과 협업의 문제들을 해결하는 데 충분한 역할을 소화해야 합니다.

When I visit client organizations, I sometimes see leaders and CEOs struggling to make their organization more cohesive, especially if those organizations are already grappling with departmental selfishness, a lack of information flow and ultimately a lack of cooperation. The more time passes without any of this being addressed, the stronger these silos become, leading to a wider and wider distance between departments.

Since the market is changing rapidly due to technological advancements, organizations need to be a unified whole in order to compete. Clients' diverse and elaborate tastes are another reason every department needs to be involved, as different departments offer different perspectives. This is why I am brought in: to devise strategies and methodologies to ensure that departments are organically and authentically converged. In my experience, if this does not happen, conflicts big or small, visible or invisible will frequently arise between departments, and miscommunication and misinformation will just make it worse. Abrasive and public arguments between leaders affect the ambience of the whole office. The competition between departments makes department leaders act obsequiously towards their bosses, which leads to office politics. All parties have always been unaware that they are actively developing the organization's silos.

As mentioned above, many leaders are rightfully anxious about this inter-departmental dissonance. However, breaking down the silos all at once is a difficult task, especially if they have become deeply entrenched. This is undoubtedly true in traditionally-structured, top-down organizations, because they were originally developed to encourage people to grow vertically, not horizontally. Thus, breaking down the silos in a top-down organization is an organizational oxymoron. What, then, should leaders do?

There are many approaches to busting silos in organizations. As Lynda Grantton, a management professor at the London Business School, wrote in the Harvard Business Review in 2007, assigning team leaders who are both task- and relationship-oriented is important. Additionally, creating a "helping" culture also helps, as IDEO, the world-renowned Design and Innovation firm, did. So does creating a casual place where people can run into each other and discuss organizational issues freely, like many IT companies have done, which is why it is a global trend. Of course, educating leaders to be more supportive of these types of efforts is a necessary foundation.

In short, we can try various methods and ideas even if there is no single silver bullet. What is more important is how to make these endeavors sustainable so that they can "stick" as organizational practices. In order to do so, organizations must consider how comfortably people will react to this change. Leaders should know that forced collaboration and forced horizontal culture is another form of hierarchy. That is why unofficial meetings drive collaborative culture more than official ones do. Furthermore, since creating an organizational culture takes time, leaders should be patient and steady. If not, hasty approaches result in unproductive and temporary events.

Companies focused on swift and powerful decision-making in the manufacturing age, but the focus of today's creativity-based competition is producing diverse ideas. Charismatic leadership worked well before, but empowering leadership is the leadership norm of today. Similarly, it would be desirable to move a higher portion of performance recognition from individuals and departments to interdepartmental collaborations and organizations as a whole.

If these silos are not successfully busted, many organizations will be still struggling, as they will be unable to find optimal business solutions, to recognize their shared goals, and above all, to respond to the market in an agile way. Collaboration is no longer an ideal. It is an indispensable organizational mission that allows for survival in the ever-growing complexities and volatilities of the global market.

질문 40 여러분의 조직 내에서 팀/부서/계열사 간 장벽 수준은 어떻다고 평가하십니까?

질문 41 팀/부서/계열사 간 장벽 수준을 낮추고자 한다면 조직 현실을 감안해볼 때 어떤 노력이 가장 효과적이라고 생각하십니까?

질문 42 협업과 소통을 촉진하기 위해 팀/부서/계열사 간 네트워킹을 강화할 수 있는 방안은 무엇입니까?

본 아티클에 대해 여러분은 개인적으로 찬성하십니까? 아니면 반대하십니까? 그 근거는 무엇입니까?

Pros(찬)	Cons(반)
✔	✔
✔	✔
✔	✔
✔	✔
✔	✔

• 본 주제에 대한 여러분의 최종 의견은 무엇입니까?

15. 존경받아 마땅한 리더들 In Defense Of 'The Old'

Leadership Insights : 갈수록 밀레니얼 세대의 차별성과 중요성은 부각되고, 기성 세대 리더의 장점은 등한시되는 경향이 있습니다. 하지만 조직의 최적화된 역량 발휘를 위해 서는 양자 모두 중요하며, 균형을 맞추려는 노력이 항상 요구됩니다.

Who do you think are more valuable to companies today: the young or the old? Based on my observation of and experience in dealing with large, medium, small and multinational companies, I believe corporations tend to value the young more.

This is chiefly because corporations are attempting to catch up with market trends and become more innovative so they can lead the industry. The same kind of thinking tends to apply when corporations try to change themselves and their cultures.

Most will agree that harmony between the old and the new is preferable. However, you'll notice that in contemporary culture, what's new is always more expensive, whereas what's old can be disposed or abandoned.

The more quickly the change happens, the more cheaply the old product will be sold. You can see a parallel phenomenon in cultural change. Many Korean companies have been trying to change their cultures, focusing in particular on narrowing the generation gap between millennials and the older generations.

What's notable here is that millennials' dispositions, tendencies and traits are treated as absolute, unchangeable qualities, which means that older generations are educated to understand, accept and co-exist with millennials, instead of millennials being educated to fit in better with everyone else. Understanding a different generation is absolutely desirable, but there has never been such a focus on the new so far in our country's corporate history.

Thus, in whatever company I visit and I visit more than 100 companies a year if the corporation tries to change its culture, the older people tend to be devalued, which makes them unmotivated.

This can impact the culture change negatively, because when something old is belittled before something new settles in, order and harmony wind up breaking down. Therefore, there should be efforts made to ensure a correct and precise diagnosis about which part of "the old" has been problematic and which part is worth keeping and should be passed on.

This is why it's so unfortunate that when corporations pursue culture change, they tend to forget the value and potential of the older people. However, any company that has grown has done so due to the efforts of the older generation who consistently stuck with the company and helped it get to where it is now.

For example, when I visited a client company, some executives complained about their positions and said, "I have worked hard for this company for decades, and was recognized for my obedience to my superiors. I showed blind loyalty to my company, I worked day and night, I was careful to distinguish between my private and public life, especially by not socializing during work hours. However, while all of this got me high scores in the past, this is no longer the case, and these values do not make me credible to the younger ones. Of course, since the younger generations do not evaluate me positively, my company also began to devalue me.

"Given this, older generations should not be made into scapegoats, since some of them laid the foundation for the company's growth. Employees who have served for a long time may still hold the core values that enabled the company to grow in the first place, and these values may not be totally useless. Helping these older employees maintain their pride means the company gets to keep something valuable and benefits from a smoother change process. Culture change cannot occur without the help of "the old."

🖊 _____

_____

_____

_____

_____

질문 43 여러분 조직에서 밀레니얼 세대와 기성 리더들 간의 관계는 얼마나 잘 형성되고 있습니까?

질문 44 여러분 조직의 밀레니얼 세대와 기성 리더들 간 상호 이해가 필요한 부분과 상호 존중해야 할 부분에는 무엇이 있습니까?

질문 45 조직 내 리더들이 밀레니얼 세대에게 전달해주어야 하는 핵심가치는 무엇입니까?

본 아티클에 대해 여러분은 개인적으로 찬성하십니까? 아니면 반대하십니까? 그 근거는 무엇입니까?

Pros(찬)	Cons(반)
✔	✔
✔	✔
✔	✔
✔	✔
✔	✔

• 본 주제에 대한 여러분의 최종 의견은 무엇입니까?

III

글로벌 기업을 만드는
조직문화

Organizational Culture

16. 영어로 시작하는 글로벌 조직문화 Global Corporate Culture – In English

> Culture Insights : 글로벌 조직문화를 만들기 위해서는 다양한 국가 출신의 인적 구성 뿐만 아니라 이를 연결해 줄 충분한 언어와 조직문화적 준비가 필요합니다. 그렇지 않다면 넘볼 수 없을 만큼 담장이 높은 집들이 한 마을에 모여 있는 것과 다르지 않습니다.

Last week, I conducted training for about 40 managers from different countries. It was the second workshop held by this company to grow potential leaders; the topic of the first workshop was coaching skills, and the topic this time was performance management.

Even though I have conducted a lot of similar trainings before, this workshop was unique in giving me a serious opportunity to think about the ways in which Korean corporations can create a global corporate culture.

This may be surprising: Why would a performance management workshop inspire this line of thinking, as opposed to a workshop on cross-cultural understanding or communication?

To begin with, the training participants were from 20 countries from many different corners of the world: the Americas; Europe; Australia; Southern, East, and West Asia; the CIS; and the Middle East. The varied backgrounds of the participants led to an equal variety of different voices and opinions on how managers should work, how they should deal with employees, and how performance should be measured and improved.

Of course, opinions are culturally relative, which means that there is no single "right" answer. However, I realized that in order for a Korean company to truly "go global," it will need to ensure that its subsidiaries in every country are aligned on these matters, in order to ensure that performance management is just and fair. Thus, it would be valuable to think about the most effective, globally-adaptable methods and strategies and how to share them. Without this, Korean companies will remain "global" only on the surface, while remaining "local" at their cores.

However, it is not enough to simply adopt these methods and strategies: I also believe that they should be taught and shared in English, in spite of the financial costs, length of time, and difficulty (due to language barriers) of doing so. A multi-cultural workforce will necessarily speak multiple languages, and English, as the most widely-spoken language in the world today, allows employees of many different backgrounds to communicate effectively and resolve issues of work effectiveness, global market responses, and global talent management and development. Take performance management as an example. Performance management is essentially about how to improve work processes. Conducting a workshop on performance management in English will allow Korean and non-Korean employees to have a shared understanding of various topics within this subject, such as evaluation methods and providing/ receiving feedback, which will lead to a decrease in the conflicts and frictions that come from cultural differences.

Typically, Korean corporations deal with foreign managers and employees as though they live in a separate house with impassable walls even if they're under the same roof. Most Korean corporations provide funding to help their employees improve their

English, but just a few companies provide training for their employees in English. Furthermore, they rarely educate their Korean and non-Korean employees in one place. How can employees improve their actual English skills without real-life use? And how can a company become global if employees from different countries are educated separately, on different subjects and with different instructors? Korean companies cannot become global without globally-aligned business management methods.

It is true that some Korean corporations will provide training courses in English when the courses are about cross-cultural understanding or global business communication. However, increasing the training opportunities through which Korean and non-Korean employees can gather and talk together about how to work more effectively will be more worthwhile than any other option. Korean companies usually emphasize their employees' general self-development; however, I think this is the time for them to begin to help their employees' global self-development. Conducting training in English can be a good start to creating a global corporate culture, as training then becomes a time when global mind-sets and solutions can be shared and tested. Without global competitiveness, the global market is not accessible.

✎ _____

_____

_____

_____

_____

질문 46 여러분의 회사는 글로벌 기업 문화에 어느 정도 가깝다고 생각하십니까? 그 이유는 무엇입니까?

질문 47 여러분의 회사가 글로벌 기업 문화를 갖추는 데 있어 가장 먼저 개선해야 하는 부분은 무엇이라고 생각하십니까?

질문 48 여러분 회사에 해외 지사나 연구소의 해외 직원과 영어로 함께 진행하는 교육 프로그램이나 문화를 만들 필요성이 있다고 보십니까?

본 아티클에 대해 여러분은 개인적으로 찬성하십니까? 아니면 반대하십니까? 그 근거는 무엇입니까?

Pros(찬)	Cons(반)
✔	✔
✔	✔
✔	✔
✔	✔
✔	✔

• 본 주제에 대한 여러분의 최종 의견은 무엇입니까?

Culture Insights : 보수적인 기업일수록, 업무 담당자에게 의사 결정권을 주지 않고 리더가 독점함으로써 주체적인 전문가로 양성하지 못하는 경향이 뚜렷합니다. 또 이는 기업 측면에서 글로벌 경쟁력을 약화시키는 결과를 가져옵니다.

Before becoming an independent consultant, I worked for corporations for 15 years. During that time, I participated in and led a lot of projects. Every time I worked with project participants who came from different departments and even careers, I saw conflict occurring between them. The main causes of these conflicts were participants' late outputs, irresponsible attitudes, and even absences from meetings.

When asked to explain themselves, the project members who had committed the blunders whether intentionally or unintentionally said that they were unable to act because they needed to receive permission from their bosses, who were the "final-decision makers." What's even more surprising about this response is that they were already managers, meaning that they had more than ten years of corporate experience and a wealth of knowledge about their fields.

Sometimes, these members even asked the project manager to persuade their bosses to cooperate with whatever the project needed because they had failed to do so. In order for a project to go forward, all departments must collaborate. However, since every department had different positions and situations, it was nearly impossible to finish projects without disruptions and fissures.

These days, when I visit client companies as a consultant, I sometimes see the same phenomenon. Many executives and CEOs I have met have expressed that they cannot understand why their employees are not enthusiastic about their work _ why they seem to take no ownership of it, and to feel no pride in it. Instead of making that work their own, they treat it as "just" something that their company has asked them to do. As a consultant, I always underline the importance of employees' having a "CEO mindset" and "behaving like they are the owner of the company" in terms of their investment and implementations of strategies. Sometimes, upon hearing this, higher-level corporate officers become upset because their employees do just the opposite: they are passive and withdrawn.

In order to figure out why this was so, I talked with the "problematic" employees during a workshop without their managers. They responded that they would love to behave "like CEOs" and become more autonomous, but that it was impossible given how little authority and decision-making power they were given. How were they expected to take ownership of something when they were not owners in the first place?

This changed my perspective. If CEOs and executives really want their employees to be more engaged and to show more self-determination, they need to be able to give their employees real power instead of empty verbal recognition. By doing so, employees will be truly empowered and will begin to behave like real owners of their company.

P&G, for example, already does this: they allow even their new hires to manage their products on their own. As a result, their new hires become committed to creating profits because of this right. Similarly, Zappos, the online shoes and clothing company, is famous for having open access to all documents and paperwork for all employees. Thus, their junior-level employees know what their senior executives are doing. Through this approach, Zappos has succeeded in creating a culture where employees believe that they know what is happening in their company and that everything is open to them regardless of their rank and title. How could you not feel like an owner of the company? Asking employees to be "empowered" without actually giving them any rights or authority is nonsensical and even cruel. If they really feel that they are respected both verbally and in practice, they will become real "CEOs" who will be willing to be responsible. Horizontal culture will only develop if all employees are truly horizontal.

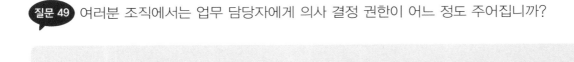

질문 49 여러분 조직에서는 업무 담당자에게 의사 결정 권한이 어느 정도 주어집니까?

질문 50 글로벌 기업 문화로 나아가기 위해 업무 담당자에게 위임하거나 의사 결정 권한을 넘겨줘야 하는 것에는 무엇이 있습니까?

질문 51 의사 결정 권한을 업무 담당자가 갖게 되면 기업 문화 측면에서 어떤 긍정적인 효과가 있다고 생각하십니까?

본 아티클에 대해 여러분은 개인적으로 찬성하십니까? 아니면 반대하십니까? 그 근거는 무엇입니까?

Pros(찬)	Cons(반)
✔	✔
✔	✔
✔	✔
✔	✔
✔	✔

• 본 주제에 대한 여러분의 최종 의견은 무엇입니까?

18. 감성 지능을 갖춘 조직문화 Emotionally Intelligent Culture

> Culture Insights : 글로벌 기업 문화일수록 조직은 수평이 되고, 성과 중심이며, 개인의 삶과 가치를 중시한다는 특징이 있습니다. 그런 면에서 직원 개개인을 중시하는 감성 지능 역량은 필수적입니다.

It does not come as a surprise that leadership creates organizational culture. For example, when leaders ignore or do not listen to their employees, nine times out of 10, their corporate culture will become a dependent culture in which employees are passive and avoid what leaders do not like.

These behavioral patterns mean that employees will not try to experiment and will remain fixated on what's traditionally been safe. Thus, for a new, desirable culture to be created, leaders must inevitably change their behavior. The biggest problem is how to achieve this change; one possible method is to increase their emotional intelligence.

Let me give you an example. Recently, I led a workshop with about 20 managers and executives, local and foreign. As part of this workshop, participants completed a diagnosis of their levels of emotional intelligence and then thought about how to improve their abilities.

In the middle of the workshop, one new senior executive came up to me and said, "I am really concerned about my emotional intelligence, and I am not sure about how to strengthen it. My leadership is self-serving, which I realize destroys team unity, and I would like to change my leadership style. My voice is always stronger than those of the others on my team, even if I don't intend it to be."

He was the manager who had had the lowest score in the assessment. This struck me because I think of him as a relatively rare leader: not a lot of leaders are willing to change, or even aware of their need to change. This resistance to change may have been acceptable in previous years, but today it is a serious impediment to organizational effectiveness.

Another example: Last year I coached two dozen executives of a large corporation on leadership skills. Their most common problem was a relatively weak ability to form a cohesive team culture. Through investigation, I found that many of them lacked strong interpersonal skills.

According to feedback from their employees, these leaders lacked consideration for others, a "human touch," an ability to understand the hearts and minds of others, and the kind of empathy that leads to mutual understanding and care.

Their strengths, on the other hand, were that they were logical, systematic and analytical. In other words, they were able to handle tasks, but not their colleagues or subordinates. Again, these skills may not have been as important even a few years ago, but today it is widely believed that a lack of these skills can destroy organizational culture.

_____

_____

_____

_____

A final example: I had another workshop with a company in which we gauged the emotional intelligence of their leaders. We looked at the four domains: self-awareness (the ability to understand one's own emotions), self-management (the ability to manage one's emotions), social awareness (the ability to understand the emotions of others) and relationship management (the ability to manage interpersonal relationships utilizing the other three domains).

For all participants, the lowest score was relationship management and the second-lowest was self-management. Even though this company actually had higher scores than many other companies, the managers agreed that they wanted to improve their emotional intelligence even further, as the organization had recently undergone a lot of structural and personnel changes, leading to widespread fatigue and stress.

It goes without saying that Korean corporations are experiencing a lot of changes due to many different factors, such as the advancement of technology, the changing dynamics of the global market, changes in the economy and in labor laws, and a shifting population composition. The more things continue to change, the more important transformational leadership will be for managers, as such ever-evolving conditions will make people feel like leaving the corporation or at least taking a rest.

For corporations to nurture a culture of cohesion, consistency and high performance, leaders must be emotionally intelligent. Constant change will result in emotional turmoil; being able to calm this will result in a more successful culture. This is why having an emotionally intelligent culture matters.

질문 52 리더로서 여러분의 감성 지능(타인의 감정을 이해하고 이에 따라 관계를 형성하는 역량) 수준은 어떠하십니까?

질문 53 리더들의 감성 지능이 높은 조직문화를 만들 수 있는 방법은 무엇입니까?

질문 54 리더들의 감성 지능 지수와 조직문화의 상관관계는 어떠하다고 생각하십니까?

본 아티클에 대해 여러분은 개인적으로 찬성하십니까? 아니면 반대하십니까? 그 근거는 무엇입니까?

Pros(찬)	Cons(반)
✔	✔
✔	✔
✔	✔
✔	✔
✔	✔

• 본 주제에 대한 여러분의 최종 의견은 무엇입니까?

19. 세 가지 나쁜 조직문화 유형 Three Negative Cultures

> Culture Insights : 조직 내 리더의 역량과 행동은 반드시 조직문화적 보상이나 희생으로 환원됩니다. 그런 면에서 과거에 쌓은 행동과 역량으로 현재를 해석하고, 현재 쌓고 있는 행동과 역량으로 미래를 예측할 수 있습니다. 만약 그 씨앗이 긍정적이라면, 그 열매도 긍정적일 것입니다.

As a consultant, I have dealt with many organizations to figure out the best approaches or strategies for solving organizational issues. Through this work, I have found some recurring negative cultures that are present in many organizations. These cultures cause people inside the organization to individually misbehave and to collectively feel negative emotions. In order to help corporations create constructive workplace cultures that will bring about greater productivity and cohesion, I would like to think about three notable negative cultures.

1) Misalignment culture
One of the most common dissatisfactions that employees have is when leadership, strategy and vision in their organizations do not function well. Employees become disappointed and discouraged when they do not know where they are headed and how they can advance. This phenomenon usually causes them to be dissatisfied with the organization, which then lowers their level of engagement; thus, this cultural malfunction has a negative impact on voluntary participation. Who would be active and willing if they did not know how what they are doing would help them? In one organization in particular, employees were complacent and rarely took risks or tried doing new things: the absence of vision led them to the conclusion that it was fruitless to try, and much smarter to simply stay idle. Many old organizations or organizations whose leadership does not try to develop its own direction or vision suffer from this negative culture.

2) Mistreatment culture

Another notable negative culture is one in which some people or departments are mistreated or marginalized. Since organizational performance is the result of interaction between people and an organizational context, any mistreatment, small or large, may well manufacture abnormal and undesirable outcomes. When these outcomes occur, it means that there is no gross internal organizational body that can control all of the employees and ensure their unity. When people are marginalized, they may suppress their resulting emotions, but no amount of suppression can get rid of these emotions entirely. Typical forms of marginalization include inequality of treatment, such as in how people of different positions are treated, in levels of compensation or recognition, or in ability to incur corporate expenses. Favoritism toward specific departments or people also tends to cause toxic problems. What's most worrisome is that this cultural rupture brings about conflicts that will end up creating organizational silos. Cultures either function or malfunction. When there are mistreated individuals or groups, this will create invisible chasms, which will consequently result in chronic disease.

3) Mismanagement culture

When employees find their workplace to be an environment that is not conducive to positive outcomes, they become suspicious of whether their CEO or leaders are truly ambitious or hopeful about the organization. Working conditions, such as systems, policies, working processes, evaluation and compensation, or talent development, engender a climate through which employees judge how promising their corporation is. If these guidelines or rules are not clear, employees will begin to doubt their corporation and begin to believe their leaders are either incompetent or uninterested. Visible inadequacy ultimately results in an invisible psychological disorder within the organization due to the absence of the principles and standards that guide and unite employees and departments. People then begin to behave according to either their own personal judgment, to guidance from trusted managers, or to the most powerful and strongest leaders. A "line" culture begins in which people queue up to get close to powerful bigwigs. Empowerment fails, and nepotism and cronyism begin growing. Companies that blindly emphasize unity, harmony and teamwork are vulnerable to this issue.

Many leaders and experts claim that corporations need to focus on creating a more successful culture. That means that corporations need to try to reframe, revamp and rebuild their existing cultures. However, entirely renovating what has been in existence is not easy, since many factors hinder the arrival of new systems. Because of this, preventing or mending some problematic cultures may help create a successful organization.

질문 55 리더들이 만드는 방향성과 비전이 조직문화에 미치는 영향은 무엇이라고 생각하십니까?

질문 56 리더들이 직원들을 존중하고, 권한을 공유하려고 하는 자세는 조직문화의 형성에 어떤 영향을 미친다고 생각하십니까?

질문 57 조직 내 공평한 기준, 원칙, 시스템을 구축하는 것은 성공적인 조직문화를 형성하는 데 어떤 영향을 미친다고 생각하십니까?

본 아티클에 대해 여러분은 개인적으로 찬성하십니까? 아니면 반대하십니까? 그 근거는 무엇입니까?

Pros(찬)	Cons(반)
✔	✔
✔	✔
✔	✔
✔	✔
✔	✔

- 본 주제에 대한 여러분의 최종 의견은 무엇입니까?

20. 생산적인 조직문화 Culture Of Productivity

Culture Insights : 생산성의 문제를 개인 역량 차원의 이슈만으로 바라보려는 것은 제한이 큽니다. 현재 조직의 일하는 방식에 대한 고찰, 지속적인 변화의 시도, 그리고 시스템을 포함한 조직문화의 개선이 보다 큰 영향을 가져올 수 있기 때문입니다.

What is happening in Korean companies? Based on a report from the Korea Productivity Center, the rate of increase in productivity has dropped drastically. In the early 2000s, the rate of increase was around 33 percent; however, it has plunged to less than 1 percent in 2016 and 2017.

Since I have been working with a company about how to increase its productivity for the past six months, I was able to think about the issue from the perspective of organizational change.

I have been surprised to see that employees do not spend a lot of time thinking about how they are working. They usually think that they should work hard, that they should work late hours, but they never question whether or not their work style is truly effective. That is why, I think, many Korean employees and managers tend to work overtime.

While absorbed in the issue, I was able to think about solutions that did not involve technological innovation or drastic cost cutting, but rather cognitive change in employees and cultural change in organizations, since I believe that these changes are more fundamental and more deeply affecting.

These types of changes can only come from strong self-awareness on the part of employees and managers, because if they don't examine themselves, they will have no idea what to change and how to change. Furthermore, leaders of an organization should approach the productivity issue from the perspective of the whole organization and its culture.

That is, the focus should be on the process instead of the result of work; changing the way people work will increase productivity.

Rather than making employees work more hours, 3M, Facebook and Google have been focusing on allowing employees more time to improve themselves, change what they are currently doing on their own, and innovate. If employees are not given these opportunities, they will simply continue doing the same thing year after year.

In order to create this kind of environment, employees and managers should be change-oriented.

Many companies tend to be satisfied when they are currently stable and peaceful. However, stability and peacefulness does not always mean that their situation is the best it can be. In fact, it might soon get worse, given that it is quite difficult to predict changes in competitors and/or external conditions.

The state of not changing means that companies are losing opportunities for improvement and value creation. Therefore, employees and managers should be able to clearly define what they are now and what they need to be in the future.

If you do not know how to change, then, the only option available to you in the future is failure. Employees and managers should remember that changing themselves results from having a strong will to change as well as being aware of any current or potential problems, and should participate in the real process of problem-solving in their own positions.

The more specific employees and managers are about what to change, the more successful companies will become. This is the starting point of productivity improvement.

Thus, companies that believe they can increase productivity permanently without changing their organizational culture through new products, for example, or through new automation systems, or simply cutting expenses and making employees work more - are mistaken.

_____

_____

_____

_____

_____

Furthermore, expecting employees and managers to drastically improve their productivity within a day is naive and unrealistic because the culture does not allow them to be innovative and productive. It is also important to keep in mind that an outward "show" of productivity is unimportant; what is important is improving employees' intrinsic commitment and engagement. Another error is to expect productivity to come from excessive self-development.

For example, a popular word, saladent, is a combination of "student" and "salaried person." Many employees were students after work, which piled yet another obligation onto their already-late nights.

The thinking was that developing employees would be helpful for their productivity and for the productivity of the company as a whole; however, in order to be truly productive, a work-life balance should be honored. If not, there may be harm to the happiness of the family, to employees' long-term stability and satisfaction in their workplaces, and to their engagement in their organizations.

That is why working effectively is more valuable than working "more." Thus, organizations should encourage employees to work more effectively through compensation, policies, and education.

This will let employees know that the quality of work is more important than the amount of work.

To create a productive work culture, leaders should be constantly attentive to their organizational health and climate, and relentlessly check whether their current culture is beneficial for quality and productivity or whether it is instead focused on excessive amounts of work. After all, leaders are at the helm.

_____

_____

_____

_____

_____

질문 58 보다 생산성 높은 조직문화를 만들기 위해서 현재 여러분 부서의 일하는 방식을 평가한다면 어떤 점수를 주시겠습니까?

질문 59 조직 내 리더들의 변화 성향과 생산성이 높은 조직문화는 어떤 연관이 있다고 생각하십니까?

질문 60 조직 건강도와 풍토를 감안해볼 때, 여러분 조직이 보다 생산성 높은 조직문화를 갖추려면 가장 먼저 개선이 필요한 부분은 무엇입니까?

본 아티클에 대해 여러분은 개인적으로 찬성하십니까? 아니면 반대하십니까? 그 근거는 무엇입니까?

Pros(찬)	Cons(반)
✔	✔
✔	✔
✔	✔
✔	✔
✔	✔

• 본 주제에 대한 여러분의 최종 의견은 무엇입니까?

Culture Insights : 고성과 문화를 직원들만 변화하면 이룰 수 있다고 생각하는 것은 착각이며, 리더의 Role Modeling이 무엇보다 중요합니다. 이는 목표 의식, 고객 관리, 마케팅, 동기부여, 갈등 관리 전반에 영향을 미쳐 고성과 문화를 자연스럽게 형성하기 때문입니다.

For the past two weeks, I have been involved in a consulting service for one of Korea's largest banks. The purpose was to examine how high-performing branches achieve their success, how they are different from medium- or low-performing branches, and how a high-performing organizational culture can be nurtured.

I visited 10 branches and interviewed their sales forces, middle managers, and branch managers. Because they were located in different environments, their answers gave me a lot of thought-provoking insights. For example, some branches told me that their remote location had prevented them from attracting customers. But location did not seem to be a problem for other remote branches.

What became most apparent was that the methods, strategies, and processes the high-performing branches adopted were surprisingly different. All had different approaches as to how sales goals should be shared with and assigned to each staff member and how comprehensive sales should be managed.

For example, some branches allocated the same share to each employee, while others only set goals for staff as a whole. Nonetheless, both types of branches had similar performances and were picked as exemplary.

Different branches also had different views about marketing, which tended to vary according to clientele and sales strategies. In addition, each branch manager had different secrets on how to motivate, educate, and manage staff. Finally, and most notably, they had different policies for sales, treating customers, and achieving sales targets.

At first, I was taken aback at how dissimilar each high-performing branch was, because I was supposed to collect common methodologies and processes that worse-performing branches could copy.

I began spending a lot of time analyzing each branch's sales trends against their strategies. However, it was not easy to find common data on what really made them excellent.

Fortunately, as the interviews went on, I was able to find what helped them some branches achieve better results than others _ the high quality of leadership at each successful branch. Even though specific techniques were different, the mind-sets, attitudes, and behavior were similar or the same.

This was my "aha moment." I was astounded by these real-life examples of powerful and influential leadership, which could be seen not only in the branches' performance, but also in how employees and middle managers talked about their branch leaders.

There were many types of effective leadership. Some leaders gave their power and influence to their middle managers, so the middle managers were the ones who really directed, motivated and educated employees.

However, some leaders took those responsibilities themselves, and showed genuine interest in how their employees were treated and what they needed. But no matter how they interacted with employees, the leaders had one thing in common: enthusiasm for their mission.

This characteristic was obvious and, because of that, had a considerable ripple effect, transferring from the top to the bottom naturally. The branch managers were role models from who middle managers and employees learned behavior.

The effects were almost magic: it seemed as though whatever the leaders wanted to happen came true. Whatever specific goals each branch had, these goals were attained.

I am not saying that the branch managers were omnipotent _ however, their leadership created an atmosphere of possibility.

Of course, they were reading their physical environments well, and creating strategies on how best to use their resources and people? Passion alone is not enough. However, their enthusiasm, keen expressions and overall attitude convinced me that the most powerful secret of high-performing organizational cultures is the spirit of their leaders.

Nowadays, many people say that Korea cannot expect the economic growth of the past due to a mismatch between the new global economic paradigm and our old, traditional approaches. But I believe that a high-performing culture is more dependent on leaders' mindsets and attitudes than on any one approach.

That is why we should look at our mental preparation and mindsets first. Then, we can look at tools, techniques and theories. Culture reflects the spirit of the leaders.

질문 61 조직들이 처한 여건이 제각각 다름에도 불구하고, 고성과를 내는 조직문화는 어떤 공통점이 있다고 생각하십니까?

질문 62 리더들이 조직문화를 형성하는 데 있어서 가장 중요한 요소는 무엇이라고 생각하십니까?

질문 63 여러분 조직이 고성과 조직문화를 구축하는 데 있어 앞으로 가장 관심을 가져야 할 부분은 무엇이라고 생각하십니까?

본 아티클에 대해 여러분은 개인적으로 찬성하십니까? 아니면 반대하십니까? 그 근거는 무엇입니까?

Pros(찬)	Cons(반)
✔	✔
✔	✔
✔	✔
✔	✔
✔	✔

- 본 주제에 대한 여러분의 최종 의견은 무엇입니까?

22. 역량 중심의 조직문화 Competency-Centric Culture(Promoting Employees' Competence)

> Culture Insights : 조직의 성장은 구성원의 성장에서 기인하며, 장기적인 로드맵 없이 조직이 성장할 수 없듯이 장기적인 비전과 플랜 없이 직원들을 성장시킬 수 없습니다. 그런 면에서 장기적으로 직원 역량을 강화하는 문화는 미래의 조직 성장에 기반이 됩니다.

For the past three or four months, I have been providing consultation for an organization to help them identify what core competencies its sales managers need to have and what their priorities should be in order to support their organization's vision and strategy. During the consultation process, I have had to make hypotheses, and I was able to test them out during the last two days of the workshop that I conducted with the sales managers. This workshop was meaningful because many sales organizations are not interested in identifying competencies for their sales managers, even though they do that for their other managers. Some sales organizations tend to focus on sales results as the sole competency and barometer for their sales managers, and the only criterion with which to decide whether they will develop their managers further. However, this excessive emphasis on sales tends to lead to a vicious circle, as Chris Argyris, an American organizational theorist, has described in his work. This circle happens because the organization's laser focus on sales will deflate the managers' appetites for growth; this lack of growth causes low productivity, which increases the company's emphasis on sales, thus beginning the circle all over again. In the end, both the organization and the sales managers lose out because neither of them is truly supporting the other.

This phenomenon is serious these days due to several factors, such as an economic slowdown, which leads to corporations having only short-term perspectives, and drastic environmental changes including unprecedented social, economic, and technological shifts. Thus, many organizations are now losing their enthusiasm for strengthening their long-term organizational or employee competencies. This negative organizational approach has the adverse effect of not motivating employees and letting them lose their initiative. What is worrisome is that when this vicious circle continues, the sense of unity between an organization and its employees will fade, the loyalty and engagement of its employees will disappear, and the organization's ability to carry out its strategy will be weakened. For this reason, how organizations view and approach their employees is key to the satisfaction of their stakeholders, including customers. This is why it is unwise to be interested only in immediate sales results.

There is no growth for either an organization or a person without increasing competencies. If you are not interested in figuring out which part of your body you would like to strengthen, how will you choose which exercises to do? This is exactly so in organizations. There are no excuses for any organization. If an organization wants to grow in future, they need to start working on a detailed implementation plan right now. Short-sightedness in organizations is dangerous for long-term growth and sustainability, because focusing on short-term profits may make the long-term perspective unclear. Thus, organizations should acknowledge that long-term vision and short-term strategy are both instrumental in becoming successful.

There is a deep connection between employees and organizations, and without employees' growth, there is no organizational growth. Given this, I think organizations should try looking deeply at what will help them remain robust in times of uncertainty, complexity and ambiguity they are dreading. How will they meet these challenges? Cutting management expenses? Introducing new technology temporarily? Harnessing a new marketing toolkit? These are all helpful, but the best defense is people, their people. To this end, I would like senior leaders of organizations to think about the three points below, which address why short-term profit should not take precedence over long-term sustainability.

First, just as it takes time for trees to grow, it takes time for employees to grow and play a primary role in leading their organizations. Employee competencies are not built in a day, so having a long-term vision for and support of employees is crucial. Second, if an organization and its employees do not envision, interpret and define their future together, the organization's overall, comprehensive competency will never become stronger. Third, in order for leaders to become true leaders, they should know how to help their employees become successful. Just asking their employees to fix their shortcomings will not help the organization prepare for the future effectively, but growing competencies will.

Since our economy has grown a lot over the past few decades, it is striking how few truly great Korean companies there are the ones that are highlighted as long-term success models. Long-term quality trumps short-term quantity in managing an organization, and sales organizations can find that long-term quality by creating a competency-centric culture. When I finished the workshop today, one sales manager told me that this is the first time he realized that his organization and he are not totally different entities but rather very intensely connected. I hope many sales organizations begin to realize their employees are the secret ingredient to building a robust future.

질문 64 직원들의 역량 구축과 조직문화의 상관관계는 무엇입니까?

질문 65 여러분 조직에서 앞으로 중점하여 개선할 직원들의 역량에는 무엇이 있습니까?

질문 66 직원 개인의 역량을 개발하는 학습 문화를 만들고자 할 경우, 여러분 조직 내 상황을 감안할 때 가장 효과적인 방법은 무엇입니까?

본 아티클에 대해 여러분은 개인적으로 찬성하십니까? 아니면 반대하십니까? 그 근거는 무엇입니까?

Pros(찬)	Cons(반)
✔	✔
✔	✔
✔	✔
✔	✔
✔	✔

- 본 주제에 대한 여러분의 최종 의견은 무엇입니까?

23. 칭찬과 인정, 그리고 수평적인 문화 Praise And Horizontal Culture

Culture Insights : 칭찬과 인정의 조직문화가 조직에 가져오는 긍정적인 효과는 매출, 생산성, 몰입도, 고객 관계 및 이직률 등 다양합니다. 하지만 수직적이고, 파괴적이며, 공격적인 문화가 이를 가로막고 있어 이에 대한 개선이 함께 이루어질 때 제대로 된 문화적 효과를 경험할 수 있습니다.

I had a recent workshop with the managers of one of the largest companies in Korea on the subject of praise and recognition culture. The managers said they already knew why praise is necessary in their organization: praise helps motivation, boosts performance achievement, and creates happy employees, which leads to a workplace that is stable and allows employees to explore their potential. It lowers stress, turn-over rates, and unnecessary conflicts.

Disney Company is well-known for implementing a praise and recognition program in which managers complimented their employees every day; this program resulted in a 15 percent increase in employee satisfaction. Similarly, according to the research done by Adrian Gostick and Chester Elton, 94.4 percent of high-morale employees out of 200,000 people surveyed over a period of 10 years said their managers were good at praising and recognizing their employees. Indeed, many studies have shown that praise results in higher productivity and a healthier culture, including a 2004 Gallup survey of 4 million people. The responses to the Gallup survey affirmed the benefits above, as well as some additional ones. Praising employees led to better relations with customersgiven that happier people tend to be kinderand thereby increased customer loyalty. Employees who received praise even had better health. If all of these things are true, praise cultures should be mandatory for organizations.

When designing this workshop, the training manager of the client company and I were concerned that the managers attending the workshop would feel awkward when practicing praise, and think that it was unrealistic to try to apply praise in the workplace, because habitual praising itself seems unnatural. We also wondered whether the managers knew who, when, and how to praise, and finally how to create a praise and recognition culture. Since this workshop was held as a direct result of a companywide survey, we were confident about its necessity.

At the beginning of the workshop, we asked the participants to discuss what praise was actually like in their workplace. Since these attendees had, on average, more than 10 or 20 years of experience as managers, their opinions were an accurate reflection of their corporate culture. On the whole, they agreed, there had been little to no praise in their workplace. We then asked them how often they personally had been praised and recognized, how their morale had been boosted, and what was stopping them from creating a praise culture.

Here is a summary of their responses:
1) The managers said that they could not provide enough praise to their employees because they did not have enough time. If you feel like you barely have enough time to get your own work done, taking time out of your day to praise your employees might feel like an unnecessary luxury. Thus, criticism was far more common than praise, as it was seen as being more necessary.

2) Sadly, the managers also said that they themselves were never praised or recognized. This means that they are actually unfamiliar with how to praise and how to be praised. As they do not know what it feels like to be praised, they cannot understand the positive impact that praise and recognition would bring.

3) Even worse, many of the mangers felt that their organizational culture implicitly devalued praise. There were four points made by their responses that supported this conclusion. ① Their performance management system focuses on finding the flaws and shortcomings of their employees. ② It is naturally taken for granted in their organization that it is the responsibility of supervisors and managers to find these flaws. However,

praise is not a part of this responsibility. ③ It is assumed in the office that employees and managers should be polite to their superiors; however, it is acceptable for them to be harsh and cold with their subordinates. Moreover, in the culture of their workplace, managers are in the habit of commanding with unilateral directives. ④ A lack of accountability allowed managers to blame subordinates instead of taking responsibility themselves. This creates the organizational assumption that the subordinates are objects to be blamed, not praised.

These responses, among many others, helped clarify why they were not motivating and encouraging their employees using praise and positive feedback. Notice that these answers were not personal. Rather, the issues stemmed from structural and cultural problems of the organization as a whole. Thus, the culture was to blame, rather than specific managers who do not praise their employees.

We do not need to try to find additional materials to prove that praise and recognition are beneficial to corporations. What is most important is how create the correct system. It is relatively easy to teach praise and recognition skills in isolation; however, it is much harder to fix an organization's deep-rooted culture. Thus, organizations should make an effort to change their rigid top-down cultures simultaneously with teaching praise skills to their managers. Praise, then, is not just a tool in and of itself: it can be a bridge to a horizontal culture that fully utilizes the strengths and competencies of its employees. Therefore, this is one of the key concepts that Korean companies should focus on in order to be more globally competitive.

질문 67 여러분 조직 내 칭찬과 인정의 조직문화는 어느 정도 형성되어 있다고 생각하십니까?

질문 68 여러분 조직 내 칭찬과 인정의 조직문화를 형성하는 데 있어서 가장 큰 장애 요소는 무엇입니까?

질문 69 칭찬과 인정의 조직문화를 만들기 위해 칭찬과 인정의 대상이 되는 직원을 찾는다면 가장 먼저 떠오르는 사람은 누구입니까?

본 아티클에 대해 여러분은 개인적으로 찬성하십니까? 아니면 반대하십니까? 그 근거는 무엇입니까?

Pros(찬)	Cons(반)
✔	✔
✔	✔
✔	✔
✔	✔
✔	✔

• 본 주제에 대한 여러분의 최종 의견은 무엇입니까?

24. 성급한 조직문화 혁신 추진 Impatient Cultural Change

Culture Insights : 조직문화의 변화는 상당히 많은 노력을 동반할 때 성공적으로 이루어집니다. 체계적인 방향에 대해 고민한 후, 사람의 중요성을 망각하지 않으면서 유연한 리더십을 발휘할 때 문화 변화에 성공할 수 있습니다.

Many organizations in Korea have recently begun to change their corporate cultures from top-down to horizontal, from organization-oriented to individual-oriented, from an emphasis on quantity of work to an emphasis on quality of work. However, many of the employees that I encounter during my work as an organizational consultant repeatedly tell me how exhausting all of these changes have been. Furthermore, they often don't even expect very much from them in terms of outcomes. Almost all of them emphasize that a culture that has taken a long time to build cannot change within a day.

If this is true and the attempt to change culture does nothing but tire out employees, why do organizations try to change their corporate cultures? Their probable intent is to achieve a better market performance or to obtain a higher satisfaction score from customers. Every effort to reach these goals is, of course, worthwhile. However, any effort to change human beings or organizations should acknowledge that the effectiveness of change has limits. If this is not taken into consideration, the new culture will become as much of a monster as the old culture was, and will make people and their organization just as powerless. In order to avoid this, change agents of organizational culture should not forget to take the following things into account when revamping their corporate cultures.

1) An obsession with perfection is a dangerous path. For example, when organizations desire to build a performance-oriented culture, they have the best of intentions. When building a culture, however, focusing on one value always comes at the expense of another competing value, so the pursuit of perfection usually has adverse effects. Becoming perfectly performance-oriented means that the value of employees as human beings is depreciated, bringing about a decline in employee engagement and commitment. An overconcentration on productivity (and efficiency, planning, and goal-setting) will also exhaust employees and lessen their senses of self-worth and empowerment. This will end up contributing negatively to long-term achievement. Additionally, this type of excessive attention to performance usually creates a phenomenon wherein organizational members either try to avoid responsibilities or push themselves so much that their pursuit of personal performance and recognition threatens to destroy organizational unity.

2) An obsession with strategy implementation makes that very implementation less flexible. This causes damage to the culture. When organizations focus too much on new products and new marketing approaches, this comes at the risk of ignoring people. In the long-term, people should drive the products, not the other way around. If employees, instead of products or marketing approaches become the targets of evaluations, the culture will overlook the importance of people's involvement and ownership. Furthermore, employees will begin to focus only on how they are evaluated and so will become merely followers and executors of whatever strategy is given to them, as opposed to being innovators. This vicious cycle will make employees less flexible than they are when they have authority and initiative, and their ability to adapt to a changing environment will decrease. As a result, employees will lose the agility and sense of empowerment necessary when penetrating into a new market. When being evaluated, people have a tendency to repeat the same behaviors as long as they are successful, which leads to an immunity to change. In this regard, it is essential for organizations to remember to value their people, as this is what creates the value of products and services.

Nevertheless, leaders are often too impatient to follow these guidelines because they think that their leadership is strong enough to change the culture quickly. That is why we should not forget that the pursuit of perfect leadership can sometimes hurt leadership. The thought that leaders should be leaders, leaders should be almighty, leaders should have all of the keys to performance can be damaging: a blind pursuit of perfect leadership can create an uncomfortable dynamic between a leader and their followers. Leadership without followers is meaningless. Group dynamics are always the foundation of group performance, especially for long-term success. Leaders erroneously think that their personal courage and determination will allow them to shine; however, strategy implementation will fail with disengaged followers.

These are just some reasons why culture change efforts should not be too rushed. Employees need leaders who put people before performance. Short-term, glorious victories do not always translate into true success. Culture change may look attractive to the leaders of organizations and push them to pursue fast transformations. However, fast transformations are apt to create fractured organizations, because it takes a long time to truly change a culture while keeping employees engaged and valued. In order to go far, walk slowly, especially for cultural change.

질문 70 조직문화를 변화시키는 것은 장기적이고 많은 노력이 필요한 과정입니다. 여러분 회사의 조직문화는 어느 정도의 변화가 필요합니까?

질문 71 많은 조직들은 핵심 가치 재정립을 통해 변화하는 환경에 맞게 조직문화를 개선합니다. 현재 업계 현황을 고려할 때 여러분 조직에 새롭게 필요한 핵심 가치가 있다면 무엇입니까?

질문 72 여러분 조직에 필요한 조직문화의 변화를 특정해 보십시오. 그리고 대략적인 절차와 일정을 만들어 보십시오.

본 아티클에 대해 여러분은 개인적으로 찬성하십니까? 아니면 반대하십니까? 그 근거는 무엇입니까?

Pros(찬)	Cons(반)
✔	✔
✔	✔
✔	✔
✔	✔
✔	✔

• 본 주제에 대한 여러분의 최종 의견은 무엇입니까?

25. 변화를 부르는 변화 이전의 변화 Change Before You Change

> Culture Insights : 개인과 조직의 변화는 현재와 미래를 객관적이고 유연하게 넘나들 수 있는 관점과 스킬을 갖고 있을 때만 가능합니다. 보다 성공적인 조직문화를 구축하는 것도 이와 같아서 리더들이 현재에 충실하면서도 미래를 늘 꿈꿀 때만 가능합니다.

At the beginning of a new year, a lot of organizations set intentions to change, just as many people do. However, as the Korean proverb says, the motivation to change only lasts three days. Why is it so difficult to overcome this inertia? I'd like to think about how organizations can start, and maintain, effective change efforts.

Many organizations and people recognize that, in order to change, we need more than the mere desire to change: we must also have analytical as well as imaginative skills. The analytical skills allow us to look at situations clearly and objectively, and the imaginative skills allow us to conceptualize what the ideal future will look like. It is important to note here that effective change does not begin only after you are changing, but rather even before you start changing. Furthermore, change requires you to change both in the middle of the change and after the change. Change is not a temporary event, but a continuous process. Here are three tactics for helping you change before you change.

First, if your organization is not clearly aware of what to and what not to change, the change has a higher risk of failing. Knowing what to and what not to change means understanding the scope, size and timing of the change; if your organization is able to do this, it is likely able to more successfully deal with the upcoming change. The more an organization is unable to draw a vivid picture of the change, the more ambiguity and uncertainty will exist. It follows, therefore, that when an organization wants to change, the information on change should be shared. If the organization is unable to share very much clear information, this is a sign that it is not ready for the change effort.

Second, organizations need to look at what they have in their hands as far as tools and skills. It is much easier to change if your organization has already had a successful change experience, but if it hasn't, it may be difficult to understand what tools, skills, and abilities are required to reach a change goal. The common assertion that change demands everyone's participation does not just mean that all of the employees and managers need to physically participate, but also that everyone needs to accept the new mindset and acquire the needed skills and knowledge. If not, the critical success factors will not be present, no matter how genuinely the change is desired. Furthermore, these new skills and knowledge may become the cornerstones or strategies through which your organization can overcome the obstacles to change. When these core competencies for change are ready, the time and cost needed for change will be reduced.

Third, organizations need to embrace opportunities to practice change whenever it arises at a day-to-day level. This means that when your organization truly needs to embark on a serious change effort, it is already experienced in making smaller changes. However, if your organization does not practice this skill, it is more likely to fail when that moment comes. Practicing how to change at a daily level means that your organization needs to look at how it is implementing change, monitor the change process and participation, and reflect on how to change the change process itself. Don't forget that the change process itself sometimes needs change and the major changes of any change process should be shared with your employees. Then, whenever it is needed in the future, change can be achieved in an easier way.

All organizations will eventually need to change at some point due to regulatory, economic, social-cultural, and technical changes in the environment. Nevertheless, changing is not easy. This is why you need to look at whether you are ready for change. Change does not happen if you have not changed before change. Change happens only when you change before change.

질문 73 조직문화를 포함한 모든 조직 변화는 준비가 매우 중요한 역할을 하게 됩니다. 그 준비 중 하나는 변화의 당위성을 만드는 것입니다. 여러분의 팀과 부서의 변화 필요성은 무엇입니까?

질문 74 여러분과 조직이 앞으로 보다 경쟁력을 갖춘 모습으로 변화한다면, 어떤 역량을 갖춘 새로운 조직문화를 갖추고 있어야 한다고 생각하십니까?

질문 75 여러분과 조직의 성공적인 변화를 위해서 설정할 수 있는 작은 목표(Small Wins)에는 어떤 것들이 있습니까?

본 아티클에 대해 여러분은 개인적으로 찬성하십니까? 아니면 반대하십니까? 그 근거는 무엇입니까?

Pros(찬)	Cons(반)
✔	✔
✔	✔
✔	✔
✔	✔
✔	✔

• 본 주제에 대한 여러분의 최종 의견은 무엇입니까?

질문 76 지금까지 아티클을 읽고 답하면서 영어에 대한 친근감을 어느 정도 느꼈나요? 영어 역량은 글로벌 리더십과 조직문화 형성에 어느 정도 중요하다고 생각하십니까?

질문 77 끝으로, 여러분 조직이 글로벌 기업이 되기 위해서 필요한 새로운 조직문화와 리더십은 어떤 모습입니까? 이를 위해 앞으로 여러분은 리더로서 어떤 노력을 해나갈 계획이십니까?

IV

글로벌 리더십과
조직문화로 나아가기

다음의 질문으로 이 책을 마치고자 한다. 우리 기업들이 글로벌 시장에서 굳건한 존재로 서려면 하루 빨리 어떤 모습을 갖추어야 할까? 나는 글로벌 조직 현장에서 다양한 면모들을 경험하고 탐색해 왔는데, 다음의 여러 가지 측면을 고려해볼 수 있을 것으로 생각된다.

우선 우리 기업 문화가 글로벌 조직문화에 부합하는지 살펴보자. 최근 들어 많이 나아지고 있음에도 불구하고 대한민국 기업들의 근로시간과 노동생산성은 지난 수십 년간 그다지 양호한 점수를 받아오지 못했다. 하지만 더 큰 문제는 이런 현상이 일시적인 제품개발과 생산만의 문제가 아니라는 데 있다. 그보다 더욱 우리의 DNA 속에 뿌리 깊게 박힌 조직문화와 인재 관리, 그리고 리더십과 팔로워십의 합작이라는 데 더 큰 문제가 숨어 있다.

생산성에 중점 하기보다는 업무를 관계 중심으로 접근하고, 협업을 지향하기보다는 내가 속한 단위 조직의 리더의 입장에 따라 움직이고, 업무를 맡고 있는 사람의 전문성 발휘보다는 조직 내 관행에 따라 의사를 결정하고, 직원들이 주체가 되기보다는 객체로서 시키는 일을 잘 해내는 능력을 평가하는 성과 관리 체계의 구습을 지적하지 않을 수 없다.

물론 한국 기업을 상대해본 외국인 임직원들을 만나보면 한국 기업 내에서도 세대 차이는 분명히 존재한다고 이야기한다. 구세대와 리더 계층보다는 젊은 세대일수록, 그리고 직급이 낮을수록 글로벌 기업 문화에 가깝다고 이야기한다. 우선 보수적 성향을 덜 갖고 있어서 타문화와 사람들, 관습의 수용에 있어 훨씬 능동적이라는 것이다. 이는 문화에 대한 오픈 성향을 증대시켜서 상호 다른 이문화 간의 융합에 긍정적인 촉매 역할을 한다고 귀띔한다. 또 젊은 세대일수록 비교적 더 수평적 마인드로 대하기 때문에 접근 가능성이 높고, 관계 형성이 용이하다는 것이다. 이런 특성들이 당연히 이문화에 대한 이해 노력을 하는 데도 순기능을 할 수밖에 없다. 그런 면에서 기성세대와 직급이 높을수록 문화적 오픈 성향, 수평적 마인드에 보다 노력을 기울일 필요가 있을 것이다. 물론 이는 당연히 특정 개인에 대한 이야기가 아니라 외국인들의 보편적인 평가에 기반하고 있음을 참고해 주기 바란다. 또 직급이 높은 기성세대들은 완숙한 경험과 지식을 보유하고 있다는 점도 높이 존경해야 할 부분일 것이다.

영어 사용 능력은 매우 껄끄러운 부분 중 하나이다. 이미 한국 기업들에는 어느 정도의 교육 수준을 자랑하는 임직원들이 대단히 많음에도 불구하고 영어 사용에 대해서 외국인들이 끊임없이 지적하고 있다는 것을 인정하지 않을 수 없다. 한국의 국력이 신장하고, 글로벌 시장에서 한국의 인지도가 매우 큰 성장을 했음에도 불구하고, 아직도 글로벌 언어는 영어라는 점, 그래서 영어 사용 능력을 높이는 것이 끊임없이 요구되고 있다는 점을 인정하지 않을 수 없다. 외국인들 중에는 한국인들의 영어 실력이 높다고 말하는 사람도 있지만, 정확한 커뮤니케이션 및 상호 원만한 업무 협조를 위해서는 한국인들의 영어 사용 능력을 높여야 할 필요성이 아직도 상당히 존재한다는 것이 중론이다. 이를 위해 영어 사용에 있어 읽고 쓰기의 정확성을 높이고, 사용 빈도를 높여서 자연스러움을 더욱 채득하는 것이 요구된다고 해도 과언이 아닐 것이다. 한국어가 영어만큼의 글로벌 언어로 자리매김할 때까지 영어 활용 능력 향상은 지속되어야 할 것이다.

그런가 하면 이문화의 중요한 측면 중 몇 가지를 반드시 숙고해볼 필요도 있다. 앞에서 이미 여러 차례 언급한 바이지만 수직성보다는 수평성, 집단주의 보다는 개인주의, 조직 중심보다는 개인의 삶에 대한 여유 존중 등이 글로벌 조직문화를 조성하는 데 있어서 반드시 감안되어야 할 요소들이다. 물론 최근 한국의 기업들이 지대한 관심을 보이고 있는 고성과 문화로의 변화도 필수적일 것이다. 이는 근로 시간 중심이 아닌 생산성 중심이며, 관계 중심이 아닌 업무 중심, 직급 중심이 아닌 역량 중심일 때 가능하다. 이런 문화적 특성들을 강점으로 가질 수 있을 때까지 지속적인 진단과 성찰, 그리고 개선 노력을 경주해야 할 것이다.

물론 글로벌 조직문화와 리더십의 추구는 하루아침에 이루어지지 않는다. 그렇기 때문에 꾸준히 개인 차원에서 노력하고, 스스로를 관찰하고 개선하며, 조직 차원으로 변화 수준을 높이려는 시도를 이어가야 할 것이다. 현재의 기업 문화로도 충분한 성과를 내고 있다고 자만하는 마음도 생각해 보아야 할 대목이다. 국내 시장의 한계, 글로벌 시장의 잠재력 등, 앞으로 글로벌 기업 문화와 리더십을 갖추어야 할 필요성은 지대하니 말이다. 한국 내 로컬 시장이 아닌 글로벌 시장이라면 당연히 글로벌 리더십과 조직문화라야 성공 확률이 높을터이니 말이다. 이제 앞으로의 성공은 글로벌 리더십과 조직문화에 달려 있음을 잊지 말자!

글로벌 기업을 만드는

조직문화와
리더십

발행일 2019년 8월 20일

지은이 김종남(John Kim)

편집책임 윤영란
디자인 김세린
마케팅 현석호, 신창식
관리 남영애, 김명희

발행처 스쿱(SKOOB)
발행인 최우진
등록일자 2013년 3월 3일
등록일자 제 2013-000236호
주소 서울시 마포구 동교로13길 34(04003)
전화 02)333-3705 · **팩스** 02)333-3748

ISBN 979-11-88871-01-8-03320

이 도서의 국립중앙도서관 출판예정도서목록(CIP)은 서지정보유통지원시스템 홈페이지(http://seoji.nl.go.kr)와
국가자료공동목록시스템(http://www.nl.go.kr/kolisnet)에서 이용하실 수 있습니다.
(CIP제어번호: CIP2019028998)